THE HIDDEN KITCHEN

PAUL GOULD

First published in 2008 by Modus Creative Limited

54 Foregate St

Worcester

WR1 1DX

11 10 09 08

1 3 5 6 4 2

Design and art direction: Modus Creative
Editor: Laura James
Food styling: Tina Boughie
Photography: Andy Davis/istockphoto.com/Oxford Blue cheese image: photographersworkshop.com

ISBN 978-0-9558601-0-2

Printed and bound in China by the Overseas Printing Corporation

To my wife, Shereen, my daughter, Katie, and my son,
Matthew, for their understanding and patience.

To my colleagues and friends at The NEC Group
for their support, friendship and ongoing pursuit of 'world-class'.

CONTENTS

All recipes are designed to serve six, but can be adapted for more or fewer guests.

FOREWORD

I've known Paul for more than 20 years...

I've known Paul for more than 20 years and count him among my circle of trusted friends and respected peers. We've seen each other a lot over the years and judged many competitions together, and I've found him to be a consummate professional. He is the epitome of a classically trained chef; cooks to the very highest standards and loves a large audience.

Paul has cooked for everyone – from an excited concert-goer to the Queen. He has a great respect for food, for the best ingredients and for continuous innovation.

Paul is an advocate of training and his team of chefs at The NEC Group is testament to this. His character is one of relentless enthusiasm and it's rare to find a man so passionate about his job. He's given much to the industry and the huge number of awards he and his team have won at culinary competitions is well deserved.

I was really pleased when I heard that Paul was writing this book; I think it's a great way for him to get his message to a wider audience. It's also an impressive way to show people what really goes on in the kitchens at The NEC Group's excellent venues and to showcase the quality of the food they produce.

I've eaten there many times, most recently at large banquets. The food has always been wonderful. Paul is one of the few chefs that can still do everything other chefs have forgotten. There's also still real theatre around his food, but – importantly – it's also delicious.

Andreas Antona
Chef Patron, Simpsons

INTRODUCTION

Very few can claim their dishes have been tried and tested by millions –
but we can...

With more than four million visitors to our venues every year, many have enjoyed our fine dining experience. In my position as Group Executive Head Chef I'm proud to bring this selection of recipes to life in *The Hidden Kitchen*.

The book aims to turn the spotlight on a well-kept secret – the wonderful food produced within the myriad kitchens of The NEC Group by a team of hugely talented chefs. I felt it was time their delicious secrets were shared.

While we are most publicly recognised for our food for visitors at the huge exhibitions and events hosted by The NEC Group, our award-winning bank of chefs has also cooked for some of the biggest names in sport, music, royalty and politics over the last 30 years.

I'm passionate about food. I love spending time selecting perfect, fresh ingredients; I enjoy the magic of shaping them to create classic and innovative recipes; and I feel real pride when I see those dishes being enjoyed. And, whether I'm cooking for a prestigious banquet for thousands at work or for my closest friends and family at home, the pleasure is just the same.

My passion for cooking was ignited around the age of eight, when I befriended an old chef in a small hotel close to where I used to live. Having lost my father when I was seven, I suspect that my lacking a father figure was clear to him. Our conversations led to me first simply peeling potatoes to help him with the Sunday roasts, and on to my persistent questioning of what he was cooking and how. I instinctively loved the atmosphere, the aromas and the activity of being in the kitchen with him and saw that a life spent in the kitchen was a "life well spent".

My next inspiration on the journey to becoming an Executive Chef came from a lecturer at the Birmingham College of Food – Ray Sayers – whose advice about the importance of gaining experience at continental, high-end London and five-star hotels became my quest for the next stage in my career, which included time at the Hotel Sonnenberg, Switzerland, the New

Berkeley Hotel in Knightsbridge and the Royal Bath Hotel in Bournemouth.

And now, after more than 30 years of change, growth and innovation at The NEC Group, the statement of it being a "life well spent" has certainly proved true for me.

In kitchens the size of ours, flexibility is key. There can be up to 85 chefs and kitchen staff around you, and visitor numbers and client demands can change at any point during the build-up to an event. The team is used to adapting and producing anything from sushi for six to a banquet for 6,000. As The NEC Group offers a wider range of dishes than any other catering establishment in the UK, our core desire is to ensure that every dining experience our audiences have with us is the best that it can possibly be.

I'm certain you will want to create the same feeling among guests to your home. That's why I firmly believe that dinner party menus should be impressive, but should not mean you need to spend hours in the kitchen instead of with your guests. The recipes we've selected for this inaugural cookery book from The NEC Group were chosen because of their popularity with our organisers and visitors.

Some are heavily weighted in terms of pre-party preparation, meaning you can get lots done in advance, while other more sophisticated recipes require greater skill and effort. So it really is true when they say that at The NEC there is something for everyone. The key to being confident in the kitchen is not being afraid to take small risks with recipes – don't be scared or nervous of getting it wrong.

This book should be used as a guide to creating innovative dishes that your guests will remember, not to be a prescriptive ruling on a recipe. All recipes here are designed to serve six, but can be adapted for more or fewer guests. If you want to try substituting haddock for salmon, or beef for lamb, I'd suggest you go ahead. Be brave, but be mindful of the need to test beforehand.

If you're a keen and confident cook already, then you may want to go through the whole process of ingredient sourcing, stock-making, pastry-kneading and wine-reducing. But if you're limited on time, don't be afraid to use ready made options, which are often very good.

To really make cooking for your guests enjoyable and worthwhile, you have to know your audience well – cooking for six close friends may be a very different experience to cooking for your work colleagues. The guests you invite will, of course, not only affect the ingredients you choose, but also how comfortable you are with making any mistakes.

When we cook for events here at The NEC Group, we only get one chance to get it absolutely right. This means having a drive for excellence, a passion for food and consistent quality control of our ingredients, equipment and service levels to ensure attention is paid to the finest details – every single time.

I see this book as a companion in the kitchen – a confidence boost to people who love cooking and want to elevate their skills and presentation to the next level. More experienced cooks can mix and match, take inspiration from these recipes and make them their own, while others will use them to stretch their own imagination and that of their guests.

I've spent years learning and perfecting my trade – travelling the world looking for new inspiration – and now manage a total of 63 kitchens and 80 staff. Being a chef isn't simply a job to me, it's a way of life, and I wouldn't change it for anything. Each day I come into work and I am grateful for having a job I love and such a brilliant team to work with.

After all, there are few things better in life than great food shared with friends.

Without doubt, the standard of food served annually by The NEC to our 1,500 hospitality guests is good enough to grace the table of any top London restaurant. It is not surprising that they have many award-winning chefs among their team.

Mark Wein
Director, Horse of the Year Show

Honey-roasted Duck Breast and Rocket Orange Salad with Plum Dressing and Spiced Plantain Crisps

There's nothing new about the combination of duck and orange, but this dish has an extra fruity element and a spicy kick.

Honey-roasted Duck Breast

3 x 200g Gressingham duck breasts

1 tsp Chinese five spice powder

Salt & pepper

30g clear honey, warmed

Honey-roasted Duck Breast

Pre-heat the oven to 160°C. Score the skin side of the duck breast in a criss-cross fashion, taking care not to cut too deeply. This will help the skin to crisp.

Heat an oven-proof, non-stick frying pan on the hob. Season each duck breast with a little Chinese five spice powder and salt & pepper. Place the duck, skin side down, in the pan and cook for about 4 minutes until golden brown. Turn over the breast and seal the other side for a further 4 minutes. Brush with warm honey and place in pre-heated oven for 10 minutes. Transfer to a plate and brush with a little more clear honey and leave to rest.

Rocket Orange Salad

2 tbsp extra-virgin olive oil

175g shiitake mushrooms, sliced

100g rocket

50g curly endive

25g red chard

125g red cherry tomatoes

15g fresh coriander

1 tbsp balsamic vinegar

3 large oranges

75g broad beans, shelled

Rocket Orange Salad

Heat 1 tbsp of olive oil in a non-stick frying pan and cook the mushrooms for 2 minutes. Allow them to cool.

Wash and tear the salad leaves and drain thoroughly. Set on kitchen roll to drain. Place them in a bowl with halved cherry tomatoes, coriander and mushrooms. Dress the salad with a little olive oil and balsamic vinegar.

Remove the skin and pith from the oranges and cut out the segments. Leave to one side. Drop the broad beans into boiling water and cook for 5 minutes. Refresh them under a cold tap. Keep aside for later, along with the oranges.

Spiced Plantain Crisps

1 under-ripe plantain (green)

1 tsp blackened Cajun seasoning

Salt & pepper

Plum Sauce Dressing

200ml jar of plum sauce

Spiced Plantain Crisps

Pre-heat the deep-fat fryer to 160°C. Peel and thinly slice the plantain into six lengthways (using a plastic mandolin will make the slicing of the plantain far easier). Place the plantain slices in the deep-fat fryer for about 3 minutes or until golden brown. Remove from the fryer and drain on a piece of kitchen paper. Dust with blackened Cajun seasoning and salt & pepper.

Plum Sauce Dressing

This can be purchased from any good high street supermarket. To make it even easier to use, warm it slightly and transfer to a squeezy bottle.

And finally…

Place a good stack of the dressed salad leaves in the middle of each of the large plates. Set the orange segments and broad beans around the edge of the leaves. Slice each duck breast into six pieces and place three slices on to each salad. Set a plantain crisp on top of the duck and ring the salad with the plum sauce dressing.

Eggs Benedict with Parma Ham
and Dolcelatté Cheese Hollandaise

A comforting classic with a twist. Perfect for informal kitchen suppers or as a starter…

Crisp Parma Ham

12 slices Parma ham

Crisp Parma Ham

Place a piece of greaseproof paper on a baking sheet. Lay six slices of the Parma ham in a row on the paper, ensuring none overlaps. Set aside the remaining six slices of ham. Place another piece of greaseproof paper on top of the ham and another baking sheet on top to weigh it down; this ensures the ham stays flat.

Pre-heat the oven to 160°C. Place the trays in the oven and cook for around 20 minutes. Remove from the oven and allow the ham to cool with the trays and paper still in place. Gently remove the crisp Parma ham, put it on a plate and set aside.

Dolcelatté Hollandaise

120ml tarragon vinegar
6 peppercorns
25g parsley
2 shallots, finely diced
300g butter
3 egg yolks
Salt & pepper
60g Dolcelatté

Dolcelatté Hollandaise

Place the vinegar, peppercorns, parsley and shallots in a small saucepan and bring to the boil. Simmer vigorously for 3 minutes, which should reduce the liquid by half. Pour the reduction through a fine sieve into a clean bowl and set aside.

Put the butter in a small saucepan, then place that pan inside a larger pan of simmering water, taking care not to get the butter wet. Wait until the butter has fully melted and then, with a ladle, take out the clear clarified butter, leaving impurities (which will be a whitish colour) in the bottom of the pan. Leave to one side to cool down slightly, but don't allow it to go cold.

Put the egg yolks in a bowl, add the salt & pepper and whisk together. Add the vinegar reduction and whisk until it's mixed together. Put the bowl over a saucepan of simmering water and continually whisk until the mixture starts to thicken and take on a creamy consistency, then remove from the heat.

Gradually add the clarified butter, whisking all the time, until all the butter has been added. This should take 6-7 minutes. Take care not to overheat the mixture or it will split. Finely crumble the Dolcelatté and whisk it into the sauce.

Poached Eggs and Muffins

10cl tarragon vinegar

6 large fresh eggs

3 white breakfast muffins

40g flat-leaf parsley

Poached Eggs and Muffins

Put a shallow-sided pan of water on the stove. Add the tarragon vinegar, bring to the boil and then lower the heat until it is gently simmering. Crack each egg into a cup and then gently place each egg in the simmering water.

Poach the eggs until the yoke is just starting to cook; this should take around 3 minutes. Carefully lift the eggs out of the water, put them aside and keep them warm.

And finally…

Toast the muffins and put half on each plate. Add a slice of uncooked ham and place a poached egg on top. Spoon over some of the Dolcelatté Hollandaise and lean the crisp, cooked Parma ham up against the side of the muffin. Finish with a little flat-leaf parsley.

Wild Mushroom and Wilted Plum Tomato with Asparagus Salad and Parmesan Crisp

An easy dish which can be prepared in advance, leaving you more time to relax…

Parmesan Crisp

90g Parmesan, grated
½ tbsp sesame seeds
½ tbsp poppy seeds

Parmesan Crisp

Pre-heat the oven to 160°C. Lay a piece of greaseproof paper on a baking sheet and divide the grated Parmesan into six 7cm diameter circles. Sprinkle the sesame and poppy seeds over the Parmesan and bake in the oven for 6 minutes or until golden brown. Take the crisps out of the oven and leave them on the tray to crisp up further. Don't remove them until they are cool.

Asparagus Salad

12 large asparagus spears
1 large red pepper
100g curly endive
50g watercress

Asparagus Salad

Cut the asparagus into 12cm lengths from the tip down. Lightly peel 2cm from the bottom, to expose the white. Place in salted boiling water for 4 minutes until just soft. Remove and put into iced water to prevent further cooking. De-seed the red pepper and cut into six large pieces. Lightly colour in a hot non-stick pan. Place the peppers on a plate and leave to cool. Pick and wash the curly endive and watercress, then drain them thoroughly on kitchen roll to remove any excess water.

Wilted Plum Tomatoes

3 large plum tomatoes
1 tbsp olive oil
1 clove of garlic, peeled
1 sprig fresh thyme
Sea salt
Cracked black pepper

Mushroom Garnish

300g wild mushrooms, brushed clean
100g button mushrooms, brushed clean
1 clove of garlic, peeled
2 tbsp extra-virgin olive oil
1 tbsp fresh tarragon, chopped
Salt & pepper

Green Herb Oil Dressing

120ml extra-virgin olive oil
1 tbsp fresh parsley, chopped
1 tbsp fresh chives, chopped
1 tbsp watercress, chopped
Salt & pepper

Wilted Plum Tomatoes

Pre-heat the oven to 110°C. Cut the plum tomatoes in half lengthways and lay them, skin side down, on a flat baking tray. Brush with olive oil. Slice the garlic thinly and place a slice on top of each tomato. Take a little thyme and put it on top of the tomatoes. Season with salt & pepper and place in the oven for 1 hour to dry them out.

Mushroom Garnish

Slice the mushrooms evenly, but not too thinly, and leave to one side. Finely chop the garlic and fry off in a little olive oil; don't allow it to brown. Add the mushrooms and the tarragon and cook for a further 4 minutes. Remove from the pan and leave to one side. Season according to taste.

Green Herb Oil Dressing

Place all the ingredients in a blender and whizz until the oil is bright green in colour and smooth in texture. Season according to taste, then pass through a strainer and transfer to a squeezy bottle.

And finally…

To assemble the dish, take the curly endive and watercress and set it in the middle of a large plate. Place the mushrooms on top. Place a wilted plum tomato on one side and a red pepper on the other, with two pieces of asparagus. Set a Parmesan crisp on top of the dish. Ring the salad with the green herb dressing and serve.

Lemon Chicken with Roasted Pine Nut Tabbouleh and Red Chard Salad

The textures and flavours of this dish make it an ever popular one for us. It looks great too, so is sure to impress your guests...

Lemon Chicken

3 x 200g skinless chicken breasts

2 tbsp extra-virgin olive oil

2 cloves of garlic, chopped

1 large lemon

1 tsp fresh tarragon, chopped

1 tsp turmeric powder

Lemon Chicken

Pre-heat the oven to 160°C. Trim off any excess fat from the chicken breasts and place in a bowl with olive oil and add the garlic. Squeeze and chop the lemon into the bowl, along with the tarragon and turmeric. Turn the chicken over in the marinade, mix well and leave to marinate for at least 4 hours in the fridge (preferably overnight).

Remove the chicken from the marinade and scrape off any excess. Heat a grill-pan on the hob, until it's very hot. Place the chicken smooth side down on the grill–pan and brand for roughly 2 minutes then lift the chicken and turn 45°. Place back on the grill-pan and cook for a further 2 minutes so that you get the "criss-cross" effect as pictured. Remove, place on a baking tray and cook in the pre-heated oven for 15 minutes. Allow to cool.

Tabbouleh Salad

250g bulgur wheat

1 litre white chicken stock
   (see page 207)

1 clove of garlic, peeled and finely
   chopped

1 red pepper, deseeded and finely
   chopped

2 tbsp fresh coriander, finely chopped

2 tbsp tarragon, finely chopped

2 tbsp parsley, finely chopped

Juice of 1 lemon

4 tbsp extra-virgin olive oil

50g pine nuts

Salt & pepper

Tabbouleh Salad

Place the bulgur wheat in a large bowl. Bring the chicken stock to the boil and add the garlic. Pour over the bulgur wheat and leave to one side for 20 minutes until all the stock has been absorbed.

Add the pepper, herbs, lemon juice and olive oil to the tabbouleh. Dry-fry the pint nuts until lightly brown. Allow them to cool before adding them to the tabbouleh. Gently turn over the whole mix with a fork. Season with salt & pepper.

Red Chard Salad

55g red chard
55g curly endive
55g rocket
2 red peppers

Sweet Chilli Dressing

50ml redcurrant jelly
100ml sweet chilli sauce (from any high
  street supermarket)
1 small red chilli, finely chopped
10g fresh mint

Red Chard Salad

Tear and wash the three lettuces and drain thoroughly on kitchen roll to remove any excess water. De-seed both red peppers and cut into 12 large pieces, then lightly colour in a hot non-stick pan. Place the peppers on a plate and leave to cool.

Sweet Chilli Dressing

Melt the redcurrant jelly in a saucepan over a medium heat. Add the sweet chilli sauce and mix together. Cut the chilli in half lengthways and remove the seeds, finely chop it and add it to the dressing. Remove the pot from the stove and allow to cool down, then add the chopped mint and transfer to a squeezy bottle.

And finally…

Divide the salad between six large serving plates and put two tablespoons of tabbouleh on top. Place two of the red pepper pieces to one side of the tabbouleh, slice each of the chicken breasts lengthways and set one half on top of the tabbouleh. Ring the salad with the sweet chilli dressing and serve.

Blackened Plum Tomato and Griddled Aubergine with Mozzarella with Herb Dressing

A vibrant, colourful summer dish with interesting flavours and textures make this perfect if you have vegetarian guests…

Blackened Plum Tomato and Griddled Aubergine

3 plum tomatoes

5 tbsp olive oil

1 clove of garlic, peeled and thinly sliced

1 sprig fresh thyme

Sea salt

Cracked black pepper

1 large aubergine

1 red pepper

1 yellow pepper

1 red onion, peeled

2 large buffalo mozzarella balls

Blackened Plum Tomato and Griddled Aubergine

Heat a large non-stick frying pan until it's smoking. Cut the plum tomatoes in half and place them, cut-side down, in the pan, then sear for 1 minute until lightly blackened. Lay them skin side down on a flat baking tray and brush with a little olive oil. Place a slice of garlic and a pinch of thyme on top of each tomato. Season with salt & pepper and place in the oven for 30 minutes to dry them out a little.

Slice the aubergine lengthways into 1cm thick pieces. Drizzle with olive oil, season and place them in a hot griddle pan. Grill both sides for about 4 minutes until they're soft and cooked through. Remove from the heat and leave to cool.

De-seed the peppers and cut them into six large pieces, then lightly brown in a hot non-stick pan. Place the peppers on a plate and leave to cool. Roughly chop the red onion into six large pieces. Heat a little olive oil in a frying pan until it is smoking and cook the onions until soft. Remove and allow them to cool.

Open and drain the mozzarella balls on a piece of kitchen roll, then place to one side for assembly of final dish.

Green Herb Oil Dressing

120ml extra-virgin olive oil
1 tbsp fresh basil, chopped
1 tbsp fresh tarragon, chopped
1 tbsp parsley, chopped
Salt & pepper

Balsamic Dressing

25cl balsamic vinegar

Focaccia Croute

1 medium focaccia loaf
1 tbsp extra-virgin olive oil
1 tbsp dried mixed herbs
Sea salt
Cracked black pepper

Salad Leaves

60g curly endive
60g iceberg
60g lollo rosso

Green Herb Oil Dressing

Place all the ingredients in a blender and whizz until the oil is bright green in colour and smooth in texture. Season according to taste, then pass through a strainer and transfer to a squeezy bottle.

Balsamic Dressing

Heat a saucepan on the hob, pour in the balsamic vinegar and reduce on a high heat for about 10 minutes, until it takes on a syrupy consistency. Remove from the heat and allow to cool, before transferring to a squeezy bottle.

Focaccia Croute

Pre-heat the oven to 160°C. Cut the focaccia into six thin slices and lay them on greaseproof paper on a baking sheet. Drizzle with olive oil and sprinkle with the mixed herbs and salt & pepper. Bake in the oven for 12 minutes until golden brown. Allow to cool.

Salad Leaves

Tear and wash the three lettuces. Drain thoroughly and set on kitchen roll to remove any excess water.

And finally…

To assemble the dish, divide the three lettuces between six large plates. Layer the aubergine, peppers and onions on top of the lettuce and place the wilted tomato to the side. Slice each mozzarella ball into six pieces and lay two pieces on top of the roasted vegetables. Squeeze a little of the green herb oil over the lettuce, vegetables and buffalo mozzarella, then lay the focaccia croute on top. Ring the salad with the balsamic dressing and serve.

Tartare of Cornish Crab with Samphire Salad and Roasted Red Pepper Dressing

Crab and samphire are a match made in heaven – a delicious light starter with flavours and textures that combine perfectly…

Tartare of Crab

500g fresh white crab meat

2 tbsp good mayonnaise

1 tbsp dill

Juice of ½ a lemon

1 tbsp fresh chives, finely chopped

Salt & pepper

Tartare of Crab

Place the crab meat on a tray and carefully feel through it to remove any shell. Place in a bowl. Add the mayonnaise, dill, lemon juice and chives and gently mix together. Season according to taste.

Spoon the mix equally into six 5cm stainless steel rings and pack tightly to remove any air pockets. Put on a plate in the fridge as this will help them to set. It's best to do this at least 6 hours before you need them, as they'll come out of the rings more easily and neatly.

Roasted Red Pepper Dressing

300g red peppers

25ml red wine vinegar

1 tbsp tomato purée

1 tbsp tomato ketchup

Salt & pepper

Roasted Red Pepper Dressing

Pre-heat the oven to 160°C. Roast the red peppers for 15 minutes. Remove the peppers and allow them to cool. Cut them in half, remove the seeds and place in a blender. Add all the other ingredients to the blender and blitz until smooth. Pass through a fine sieve and allow it to cool, then put into a squeezy bottle in the fridge.

Parmesan Crisp

90g Parmesan, grated

½ tbsp sesame seeds

½ tbsp poppy seeds

Parmesan Crisp

Pre-heat the oven to 160°C. Lay a piece of greaseproof paper on a baking sheet and divide the grated Parmesan into six 7cm diameter circles. Sprinkle the sesame and poppy seeds over the Parmesan and bake in oven for 6 minutes, or until golden brown. Take the crisps out of the oven and leave them on the tray to crispen further. Don't remove until they are cool.

Samphire Salad

2 large eggs
30g small capers, well drained
30g shallots
1 tbsp dill
1 tbsp chives
3 quail's eggs
150g fresh samphire
Crushed black pepper

Samphire Salad

Hard-boil the eggs and let them go cold. Remove the shells and chop them into very small dice. Place them in a bowl with the capers. Finely chop the shallots, dill and chives and gently combine with the egg mix.

Bring a very small pan of water to the boil and add the quail's eggs. Boil for 2 minutes, so they are just hard-boiled. When they're ready, put them into a bowl of iced water for 10 minutes to prevent them over-cooking. Carefully peel them, cut them in half and place in the fridge until needed.

Put the samphire in a pan of unsalted boiling water and cook for 1 minute. Drain and then put it into a bowl of iced water. This will ensure it retains its crispness and dark green colour.

And finally…

Squeeze a tablespoon of the roasted red pepper dressing at the centre of six large plates. Then take the crab out of the fridge. Roll the mould in the palm of your hands just to slightly warm it and gently press the crab down on to the red pepper dressing, carefully removing the ring. Place the Parmesan crisp on top of the crab. Drain the samphire. Season with the pepper and place it on top of the Parmesan crisp with half a quail's egg. Set the egg, herb, caper and shallot mix round the edge of the plate, circling the crab as pictured.

Chef's tip

Samphire can be bought from most good fishmongers, but if it's not available then fine baby asparagus will work just as well. Simply cook it in the same way as the samphire.

Char-grilled Squid with Saffron and Sweet Bell Pepper Linguine and Lobster Sauce

Rich in colour, textures and flavours, this dish will have real impact for your guests. The pangritata adds interest and a delicious crunch…

Fresh Lobster

1 x 450g live lobster

Fresh Lobster

Bring a large pan of salted water to the boil. Place the live lobster in the water and boil for 6-8 minutes. Remove the lobster from the pan, place it on a tray and cover with a damp cloth. When it's cool, refrigerate it for 1 hour. To prepare the lobster, remove the tail and the claws using kitchen scissors. Snip the underside of the tail, pull the shell apart and remove the tail meat. Wrap the claws in a cloth. To crack them, gently tap them with a rolling pin or a small hammer. Carefully remove the meat from the claws, ensuring there's no shell left in the claw meat. Dice the claw and tail meat neatly and refrigerate until needed. Meanwhile, crush the lobster head and shell with a rolling pin or small hammer until the pieces are as small as possible. Set aside the crushed shell to use in the sauce.

Lobster Sauce

1 tbsp olive oil

2 large carrots, peeled and chopped

4 shallots, peeled and chopped

2 celery sticks, chopped

1 white leek, diced

½ fennel bulb, diced

1 clove of garlic, crushed

A few fresh basil leaves

A few fresh tarragon leaves

1 tbsp tomato purée

6 plum tomatoes, quartered

Crushed lobster shell (prepared earlier)

1 tbsp brandy

300ml white wine

1.75 litres fish stock (see page 208)

50g long grain rice

100ml double cream

Juice of ½ a lemon

Salt & pepper

Lobster Sauce

Heat the olive oil in a large saucepan and add the carrots, shallots, celery, leek, fennel, garlic, basil and tarragon. Gently cook until they are lightly coloured. Add the tomato purée and the tomatoes and cook for a further 2 minutes.

Add the crushed lobster shell and cook for a further 2 minutes. Add the brandy and white wine and reduce by half. Add the fish stock, bring to the boil and then simmer for 20 minutes.

Add the rice and simmer for a further 20-25 minutes. The rice needs to be overcooked to enable the sauce to thicken. Remove from heat then pour all the sauce, including the lobster shells, into a liquidiser and blitz. Pass the sauce through a fine strainer into a saucepan. Add the cream and lemon juice and season with salt & pepper. A good way to check the sauce is the right consistency is to ensure it coats the back of a stainless steel spoon. If it's too thick, add a little water.

Char-grilled Squid

500g squid tubes (available cleaned from
  good fishmongers)
2 tbsp olive oil
1 clove of garlic, peeled and crushed

Pangritata

1 small foccacia loaf
1 tbsp extra-virgin olive oil
1 tsp dried mixed herbs
Sea salt
Cracked black pepper

Linguine

350g dried linguine
1 tbsp olive oil
1 red chilli, finely chopped
100g pepperdillos
100g baby asparagus
Pinch of saffron
1 tbsp chives, chopped
Lobster meat (prepared earlier)
Marinated squid (prepared earlier)
Salt & pepper

Char-grilled Squid

Remove the transparent cartilage from the body of the squid and wash the remaining tube. Dry well and cut the tube in half. Using a sharp knife, lightly score on both sides. Combine the olive oil and garlic in a bowl, then add the squid tubes and marinade for 20 minutes.

Pangritata

Pre-heat the oven to 160°C. Thinly slice the foccacia, then lay it on a greased tray and drizzle with olive oil. Sprinkle with the mixed herbs, the sea salt and a twist of black pepper, then bake in the oven for 12-15 minutes until golden brown. Remove from the oven, allow it to cool and break into bite-sized pieces.

Linguine

Cook the linguine in a medium pan of salted boiling water for 7-8 minutes, until al dente. Meanwhile, heat a large frying pan, drizzle with olive oil and gently cook the chopped chilli, pepperdillos and asparagus for 1 minute. Drain the linguine through a colander and add it to the mixture. Add the saffron and the diced lobster meat. Add the chives, drizzle with olive oil and season.

Pre-heat a grill-pan until it's smoking. Remove the garlic and excess oil from the squid. Griddle for 1 minute on each side and remove from the heat. Ensure you don't overcook the squid as it will become tough.

And finally…

Place a pile of linguine on to each of six warm medium bowls and arrange the mixture. Gently warm the sauce and spoon over the linguine. Place the char-grilled squid on top of the linguine, sprinkle with the pangritata and serve.

San Francisco Crab with Cioppino Soup and Saffron Aioli

A soup for all seasons, this array of flavours creates a dish that is both wholesome and satisfying...

Cioppino Soup

3 red peppers

1 medium red onion

350g plum tomatoes

2 cloves of garlic, peeled

1 tbsp olive oil

Salt & pepper

1 litre fish stock (see page 208)

100g cod fillet, skinned and pin-boned

1 tbsp tomato purée

1 sprig fresh oregano

250g tinned chopped tomatoes

1 tbsp sweet chilli sauce

Seafood Island

1 tbsp olive oil

1 red pepper, de-seeded and finely cut

1 yellow pepper, de-seeded and
 finely cut

100g cooked mussel meat, chopped

80g cooked white crab meat, chopped

100g peeled cooked prawns, chopped

1 tbsp coriander, chopped

1 tbsp fresh chives, chopped

Cioppino Soup

Pre-heat the oven to 160°C. De-seed and roughly chop the peppers. Peel and chop the red onion, cut the plum tomatoes in half and chop the garlic. Put all these ingredients on a roasting tray, drizzle with olive oil, season with salt & pepper and roast in the oven for 30 minutes.

Bring the fish stock to the boil in a medium saucepan. Add the cod fillet and simmer for 5 minutes, then remove the cod and keep it warm. Remove the roasted vegetables from the oven and spoon into the stock. Add the tomato purée, oregano, tinned tomatoes and sweet chilli sauce. Bring to the boil and simmer for 15 minutes.

Blend the soup with a hand blender and pass through a sieve into a clean saucepan. Season and keep it warm.

Seafood Island

Drizzle the olive oil into a hot frying pan, add the finely cut peppers and sauté for 2 minutes until soft. Add the crab meat, mussels, prawns and herbs and cook for 2 minutes until hot. Remove from the heat and keep it warm.

Saffron Aioli

50g Desirée potatoes
2 medium eggs
2 cloves of garlic, peeled
Pinch of saffron
60ml olive oil

Focaccia Croute

1 medium focaccia loaf
1 tbsp extra-virgin olive oil
1 tbsp dried mixed herbs
Sea salt
Cracked black pepper

Saffron Aioli

Peel the potatoes and cut into large cubes, then place them in a saucepan. Cover with cold water and bring to the boil. Cook until tender, then drain and allow to cool. Boil the eggs for 5 minutes until hard-boiled then cool under cold running water. Peel the eggs and remove the yolk, discarding the egg whites. Place the potato, garlic, saffron and cooked egg yolk into a food processor and blend until smooth, gradually adding the olive oil a little at a time. The aioli should be a smooth mayonnaise consistency. Refrigerate until you need it.

Focaccia Croute

Pre-heat the oven to 160°C. Cut the foccacia into six thin slices and lay them on a piece of greaseproof paper on a baking sheet. Drizzle with olive oil and sprinkle with the mixed herbs, sea salt and cracked black pepper. Bake in the oven for 12 minutes until golden brown. Allow to cool on the side.

And finally…

Ladle the soup into six shallow soup bowls. Place the 'island' ingredients into the centre of each bowl. Place a teaspoon of saffron aioli on top and finish with a focaccia croute and chopped chives.

Salad of Charentais Melon, Papaya and Mango with Maracuya Sorbet and Ricotta and Chilli Cannelloni

These refreshing tropical tastes are perfect for summer dinner parties...

Maracuya Sorbet

8 passion fruit

2 ripe mangoes, peeled, stone removed

350ml water

175g caster sugar

Ricotta and Chilli Cannelloni

170g ricotta cheese

1 tbsp caster sugar

1 tbsp fresh mint

½ red chilli pepper, de-seeded

3 pieces spring roll pastry

1 large egg, beaten

Maracuya Sorbet

Cut six passion fruit in half and scoop all the flesh into a strainer. Collect all the juice and discard the seeds. Keep two passion fruit to one side to use later. Put the mangoes and the rest of the passion fruit into a blender and whizz until it becomes a purée. Transfer to a bowl. Put the water and sugar in a small saucepan and heat until all the sugar dissolves. Remove from the heat and allow it to cool before placing in a bowl in the fridge. Once it's chilled, add the mango and passion fruit purée to the sugar syrup and pour the mixture into an ice cream machine. Churn the mixture until it is almost firm, then transfer to a suitable container and place in the freezer.

Ricotta and Chilli Cannelloni

In a bowl, mix the ricotta cheese, sugar and mint. Finely chop the chilli pepper, add it to the rest of the mix and put in the fridge until it is needed to assemble the spring rolls.

Take a piece of spring roll pastry and cut into 20cm x 10cm strips. At one end of the pastry place 1 tbsp of the ricotta mix, leaving 3cm of pastry at either side. Brush all the sides with egg wash and roll the pastry halfway up. Fold over the sides, brush the folded sides and top of the pastry with more egg wash and continue rolling so the ends become sealed as pictured. Place in the fridge to firm up.

Salad of Charentais Melon, Papaya and Mango

1 ripe mango, peeled, stone removed

1 ripe papaya

1 ripe Charentais melon

1 tsp poppy seeds

Salad of Charentais Melon, Papaya and Mango

Thinly slice the mango and cut into dice ½cm by ½cm. Peel the papaya, cut in half and remove the seeds with a teaspoon. Slice thinly and then cut into dice ½cm by ½cm. Peel the melon, cut it in half and scoop out the seeds. Slice it thinly and then cut into dice ½cm by ½cm.

Place all the diced fruit in a colander to allow the excess juice to drain off. Then place the fruit in a bowl, gently mix in the poppy seeds and pack generously into six 5cm stainless steel rings. Place in the fridge. You should try and do this at least 5 hours before you intend to serve them so they will leave the moulds neatly.

Blackened Pineapple

1 baby pineapple

1 tbsp icing sugar

Blackened Pineapple

Cut the top, bottom and all around the pineapple to ensure all the skin is removed. Cut in half lengthways and then again so you are left with four quarters, then remove the core. Cut into six equal pieces, dust with icing sugar and place under the grill for 2 minutes until it is lightly blackened and remove from grill (you can use a blowtorch if you have one).

Redcurrant and Mint Syrup

100g redcurrant jelly

70g clear honey

60ml water

1 tbsp mint, finely chopped

Redcurrant and Mint Syrup

Cook the redcurrant jelly, honey and water over a low heat for about 15 minutes until it becomes a syrup. Remove from the heat and allow it to cool. Add the mint and transfer to a squeezy bottle.

And finally...

1 tbsp icing sugar

And finally…

Pre-heat a deep-fat fryer to 170°C. Deep-fry the cannelloni until it's golden brown. Place on a metal tray, dust with a little of the icing sugar and caramelise under a hot grill for about 1 minute (you can use a blow torch if you have one). Remove and set to one side.

Place the melon moulds on six large plates and then gently remove the rings. Set the blackened pineapple against the melon and lean the cannelloni against the pineapple. Take a scoop of the sorbet and set it into a small crockery dish, then dress it with the juice and the seeds from the two remaining passion fruit and place alongside the cannelloni. Squeeze the sauce around as pictured and serve.

Seared Tuna Carpaccio Salad with Olive Oil and Beetroot Dressing

The delicate flavour of the dressing married with the clean taste of the tuna makes this dish simply delicious…

Seared Tuna Carpaccio

75g sea salt

40g caster sugar

500g tuna loin, skin removed

1 tbsp olive oil

1 tbsp Dijon mustard

1 red chilli, finely diced

1 tbsp coriander, chopped

1 tbsp dill, chopped

1 tbsp parsley, chopped

Zest of 1 lemon

Seared Tuna Carpaccio

Mix the sea salt and caster sugar together, sprinkle on to a tray and press over the tuna until completely covered. Cover with clingfilm and refrigerate for two hours. Remove the sea salt and caster sugar from the tuna loin and wipe clean with a damp cloth.

Heat a medium frying pan. Drizzle with olive oil and sear the tuna loin on all sides for about 20 seconds. Place on a tray and refrigerate until cold.

When cold, coat the tuna loin with the Dijon mustard and sprinkle with the chilli, herbs and lemon zest, coating all sides evenly. Wrap tightly in clingfilm and place in the deep freeze for 2 hours until semi-frozen (this will make it easier to slice when serving).

Beetroot Dressing

100g fresh cooked beetroot

50g redcurrant jelly

1 tbsp red wine

1 tbsp Demerara sugar

200ml water

Beetroot Dressing

Peel the beetroot and roughly chop. Place in a small saucepan and add the other ingredients. Bring to the boil and reduce by half. Pass through a fine strainer and chill.

Green Herb Olive Oil

120ml extra-virgin olive oil
1 tbsp fresh basil, chopped
1 tbsp fresh tarragon, chopped
1 tbsp parsley, chopped
Salt & pepper

Mizuna, Endive and Beetroot Salad

200g fresh beetroot
½ red pepper
½ yellow pepper
1 small curly endive
25g red chard
50g mizuna

Green Herb Olive Oil

Place all the ingredients in a blender and whizz until the oil is smooth and bright green in colour. Season according to taste, then pass through a strainer and set to one side.

Mizuna, Endive and Beetroot Salad

To cook the beetroot, place it in a small saucepan and cover with cold water. Bring to the boil and cook, covered, for 45 minutes. When cooked, remove from the heat and place under cold running water for around 5 minutes. Remove the skin and cut into 18 equal wedges.

Remove the seeds from the peppers and cut into thin strips. Wash the leaves and pat dry on kitchen roll.

And finally…

Leaving the clingfilm on, use a sharp knife to cut the tuna (it will give you a better shape) into very thin slices, around five slices per plate – ensuring you remove the clingfilm from each slice before serving!

Neatly arrange the tuna slices in the centre of each chilled serving plate. Mix the leaves and peppers in a bowl and place a neat pile on the centre of the tuna. Arrange three wedges of beetroot around the leaves, then drizzle with the beetroot dressing, the green herb oil and serve.

Smoked Salmon and Turmeric Monkfish Salad with Guacamole

This dish was first served to me in a rustic Italian fashion and tasted amazing. It's one of my favourite dishes to cook at home…

Turmeric Monkfish

480g monkfish fillets, skinned

20g dried turmeric

2 tbsp extra-virgin olive oil

Salt & pepper

Turmeric Monkfish

Pre-heat the oven to 150°C. Take the monkfish fillets and, with a sharp knife, carefully remove any black marking. Lightly dust with turmeric on both sides, season with salt & pepper and set to one side.

Place a large non-stick, ovenproof frying pan on the hob with the olive oil until it is smoking. Add the monkfish to the pan and cook on both sides until it is golden brown all over. Transfer the monkfish (in the pan) to the oven and cook for 8-10 minutes. Take out and set aside until required.

Guacamole Dressing

2 ripe avocados

1 clove of garlic, peeled

1 tbsp fresh coriander

3 plum tomatoes

2 spring onions

Juice of 1 lemon

1 red chilli, diced

Salt & pepper

Guacamole Dressing

Peel the avocado and remove the stone. Place all the ingredients in a blender and mix until you have a smooth green paste. The mixture will need thinning down. Add a little water until the sauce takes on the consistency of double cream. Season to taste, then pass through a fine strainer and transfer to a squeezy bottle. Place in the fridge until needed.

Parmesan Sables

100g plain flour

150g Parmesan, grated

75g unsalted butter

1 egg yolk

1 tsp sesame seeds

1 tsp poppy seeds

Salad

2 bunches watercress

125g red chard

125g curly endive

12 sun-blushed tomatoes

And finally…

350g oak-smoked salmon, sliced

Parmesan Sables

Pre-heat oven to 160°C. In a bowl, mix together the flour and the Parmesan cheese. Rub in the butter until it's evenly mixed. Add the egg yolk and mix until a dough is formed. Wrap it in clingfilm and leave to rest for at least 2 hours (preferably overnight).

Roll out the dough on a lightly floured surface take the dough until it's 3mm deep. Cut the dough into 6 rectangles roughly 4-8cm long. Lay them on greaseproof paper on a flat baking tray. Sprinkle over the sesame seeds and poppy seeds and bake in the oven for 15 minutes or until golden brown. Take out and allow to cool on a baking tray.

Salad

Tear and wash the salad leaves, drain thoroughly and set on kitchen roll to remove any excess water.

And finally…

To assemble the dish, divide the lettuces between six large plates and place the sun-blushed tomatoes around the edge. Take the monkfish and cut it into 12 equal pieces and place two pieces on either side of the lettuce. Divide the smoked salmon into six portions and place on top of the lettuce and set one of the sable biscuits on top of the salmon. Ring the salad with the guacamole dressing and serve.

Parma Ham Bruschetta with Baby Mozzarella, Bell Pepper Salad, Crisp Parma Ham and Aged Balsamic Dressing

The colours and flavours of Italy combine to create a light and refreshing starter...

 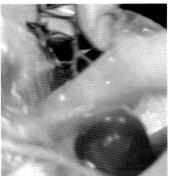

Bell Pepper Salad

200g curly endive

30g rocket

30g red chard

100g cherry bell peppers, in jar

75g red cherry tomatoes, halved

1 yellow pepper

150g sun-blushed tomatoes

Bruschetta

1 clove of garlic, peeled and
 very finely chopped

1 tbsp extra-virgin olive oil

1 small ciabatta

Bell Pepper Salad

Tear and wash the salad leaves and drain thoroughly. Set on kitchen roll to remove any excess water. De-seed the yellow pepper, cut into rustic pieces and dry-fry in a non-stick frying pan until lightly coloured. Remove the peppers from the pan and allow to cool. Drain the bell peppers and put them in a bowl with the cherry tomatoes, sun-blushed tomatoes, yellow pepper pieces and the salad leaves. Gently toss the ingredients together.

Bruschetta

Mix the garlic into the olive oil. Slice the ciabatta at an angle 1.5cm thick. Drizzle with a little garlic olive oil, place in a hot grill pan and lightly brand on either side.

Crisp Parma Ham

12 slices Parma ham

Crisp Parma Ham

Place a piece of greaseproof paper on a baking sheet. Lay six slices of the Parma ham in a row on the paper, ensuring none overlaps. Set aside the remaining six slices of ham.

Place another piece of greaseproof paper on top of the ham and another baking sheet on top to weigh it down; this ensures the ham stays flat.

Pre-heat the oven to 140°C. Place the trays in the oven and cook for around 20-25 minutes. Remove from the oven and allow the ham to cool on the trays, the paper still in place. Gently remove the crisp Parma ham, put on a plate and set aside.

Balsamic Dressing

25cl balsamic vinegar

Balsamic Dressing

Heat a saucepan on the hob. Pour in the balsamic vinegar and reduce on a high heat for 5 mintues, until it takes on a syrupy consitency. Remove from the heat and allow to cool before transfering to a squeezy bottle.

Baby Mozzarella

250g baby mozzarella

Baby Mozzarella

Drain the baby mozzarella and set on kitchen roll.

And finally…

Place a ciabatta slice in the middle of a large plate. Take the salad and arrange as pictured. Fold one piece of Parma ham in half and set to one side of the salad. Take the Parma ham crisp and set on top of the salad and place the baby mozzarella around the edge. Ring the salad with the balsamic dressing as shown.

Salmon and Prawn Assiette with Coriander Noodles and Lime and Tomato Salsa

Contemporary, delicious and impressive, this is my take on the humble prawn cocktail…

Tartare of Smoked Salmon

200g smoked salmon fillet

5 sprigs fresh dill

4 sun-blushed tomatoes

3 quail's eggs

Seared Salmon and Coriander Noodle Salad

350g salmon fillet

Olive oil for frying

200g rice vermicelli noodles

1 tbsp turmeric

1 tbsp fresh coriander, chopped

Tartare of Smoked Salmon

Dice the smoked salmon into ½cm pieces and place in a bowl. Finely chop the dill and add to the salmon, mixing it together. Place six 5cm stainless-steel rings on a plate and fill each three-quarters full of the salmon mix, making sure you push it down tightly. Leave in the fridge for at least 6 hours, preferably overnight. This means that when you turn it out, it won't fall apart.

Bring a very small pan of water to the boil and add the quail's eggs. Boil for 2 minutes, so they are just hard-boiled. When they're done, put them in a bowl of iced water for 10 minutes to prevent them over-cooking. Then carefully peel them, cut in half and place them in the fridge until needed.

Seared Salmon and Coriander Noodle Salad

Cut the salmon into six equal squares and set to one side. Heat the olive oil in a non-stick frying pan. When it's smoking, add the salmon fillets and cook on each side until the top is golden brown. This should take about 5 minutes. Remove the pan from the heat, but leave the salmon in as it will continue to cook. When the salmon is cool to the touch, transfer to a plate and place in the fridge.

Place the noodles and turmeric in a bowl and just cover with boiling water. Allow to soak for 10 minutes or until the noodles are soft.

Drain the noodles and run under a cold tap for a few minutes. Place in a bowl with the chopped coriander and put in the fridge.

Prawn Cocktail

3 tbsp mayonnaise

1 tbsp tomato ketchup

1 tsp Worcestershire sauce

350g fresh peeled prawns

6 king prawns, cooked

Parmesan Crisp

90g Parmesan, grated

½ tbsp sesame seeds

½ tbsp poppy seeds

Lime and Tomato Salsa

1 red onion, peeled

4 plum tomatoes

Juice of 2 limes

1 tbsp fresh coriander

60ml extra-virgin olive oil

1 lime, cut into six

Prawn Cocktail

Mix the mayonnaise, tomato ketchup and Worcestershire sauce in a dish. Add the peeled prawns, gently mix them up and place equal amounts into six shot glasses. Place in the fridge until needed. Peel the king prawns, removing the head, shell and membrane that runs down the back, taking care not to remove the tail end. Place in the fridge until needed.

Parmesan Crisp

Pre-heat the oven to 160°C. Lay a piece of greaseproof paper on a baking sheet and divide the grated Parmesan into six 8cm diameter circles. Sprinkle the sesame seeds and poppy seeds over the Parmesan and bake in the oven for 6 minutes, or until golden brown. Take the crisp out of the oven and leave them on the tray to crisp up further. Don't remove them until they are cool.

Lime and Tomato Salsa

Dice the red onion and place in a bowl. Quarter the plum tomatoes, remove the seeds, dice them and add them to the red onions. Pour the lime juice into the bowl and add the chopped coriander and olive oil. Mix well and transfer into six 6cm ramekins.

And finally…

Take six large plates and place a small pile of noodles to one corner of each plate. Place one piece of the salmon on to the noodles. In the opposite corner, place one of the prawn cocktail-filled shot glasses with a Parmesan biscuit on top, finished with a king prawn.

Take the tartare of smoked salmon – still in the ring – and place it in the third corner and gently lift off the ring. Place a tomato and halved quail's egg on the tartare of salmon. In the final corner, add the salsa with a piece of lime on top.

Chilli and Lime-cured Salmon with a Basil and Artichoke Frittata

The chillies and lime really bring out the full flavour of the salmon, while the frittata adds delicious substance…

Cured Chilli and Lime Salmon

350g salmon fillet, skinless and pin-boned
75g sea salt
40g caster sugar
3 limes
40g red chilli peppers

Cured Chilli and Lime Salmon

To start the curing process, place the salmon on a tray, cover with the sea salt and sugar so both sides of the salmon are covered with a thick layer. Cover with clingfilm and leave in the fridge overnight.

The next day, wash off any excess salt and sugar and dry off on kitchen roll. Squeeze the limes and pour the juice over the salmon. Cut the chillies lengthways and discard the seeds. Finely chop and spread the chillies on the top of the salmon. Place in the fridge until needed.

Basil and Artichoke Frittata

150g courgettes
75g new potatoes, skins on
1 x 275g tin artichoke hearts
1 red chilli
80g shallots
2 cloves of garlic
1 tbsp extra-virgin olive oil
1 tbsp fresh basil
1 tbsp fresh coriander
1 whole egg
Salt & pepper

Basil and Artichoke Frittata

Grate the courgettes into a medium colander. Sprinkle with a little salt and leave for 15 minutes to draw out the moisture. Place the courgettes on a clean tea towel and gently twist until most of the moisture is out. Then place the squeezed courgettes in a bowl.

Cook the new potatoes in salted boiling water until they are tender, drain well, then crush gently and add to the courgettes. Drain and chop the artichoke hearts and put them with the other ingredients. Cut the chilli lengthways, discard the seeds, finely chop and place in the bowl. Peel and finely chop the shallots and garlic and gently fry in a little olive oil for 2 minutes. Remove from pan and allow to cool before adding them to the bowl with the other ingredients.

Chop the basil and coriander, add to the bowl and mix together with the whole egg. Season to taste.

Take the mix and divide into six even balls. Flatten out to 1cm thick on greaseproof paper. Place a medium non-stick frying pan on a medium heat. Add a little olive oil and pan-fry the frittata until golden brown on both sides. Take out of the pan, place on a plate and put in a warm oven.

White Balsamic and Lemon Dressing

25cl white balsamic vinegar

1 tbsp caster sugar

Juice of 1 lemon

½ tsp black sesame seeds

Mixed Leaf Salad

100g rocket

50g curly endive

50g red chard

50g seedless green grapes

50g Borlotti beans

60g caper berries with stalks

White Balsamic and Lemon Dressing

Heat a saucepan on the hob, pour in the white balsamic vinegar and reduce on a high heat for about 10 minutes until it takes on a syrupy consistency. Add the sugar and lemon juice. Remove from the heat and allow to cool, then add the sesame seeds and transfer to a squeezy bottle.

Mixed Leaf Salad

Wash all the salad leaves and cut the grapes and beans in half and keep to one side.

And finally…

Take the warm frittatas and place them in the middle of six large plates. Slice the cured salmon thinly and layer mixed leaf salad and salmon alternately. Top with two caper berries. Place the grapes, Borlotti beans and caper berries evenly around each plate. Ring the salad with the balsamic and lemon dressing and serve.

Seared Scallops with Roasted Capsicum and Tomato Terrine

A clean and refreshing dish, just perfect for summer dinner parties...

Roasted Capsicum and Tomato Terrine

1.1kg red peppers

1.1kg ripe plum tomatoes

1 bunch basil

Salt & pepper

Roasted Capsicum and Tomato Terrine

Line a 15cm x 8cm x 8cm terrine or a loaf tin of similar size with clingfilm. Ensure it is in all the corners and that there are no air pockets. Leave an overhang of 5cm on each side. Pre-heat the grill until it's hot and grill the peppers on all sides until blackened and blistered. Allow the peppers to cool. When cool, peel the peppers, remove all the seeds and then cut them into quarters. Do not wash the peppers as their natural sugars help to set the terrine.

Bring to the boil a large pan of water. Using a sharp knife, remove the eye from the plum tomatoes and plunge them into the boiling water for 10 seconds. Remove them from the water and place in a bowl of iced water. When the tomatoes have cooled, remove the skin. Cut the tomatoes into quarters and remove the seeds. Pick the leaves from the basil and discard the stems.

Place one layer of red peppers in the bottom of the terrine, ensuring all the corners are covered. Season with salt & pepper. Follow this with a layer of tomatoes, again seasoning, then a layer of basil. Press down with your hands to ensure excess air is removed. Then repeat this step with another layer of peppers, seasoning and layer of tomatoes, which you should also season, and then the basil until you have used all the peppers, tomato and basil.

Once the terrine is filled, wrap the overhanging clingfilm over the top of the terrine and press down firmly. Place on top a wooden block, wrapped in clingfilm, which just fits the top of the terrine. Place a large weight of roughly 2kg on top. Leave the terrine with the weight on top for at least 24 hours in the fridge.

Lemon and Tarragon Oil

1 tbsp caster sugar

Juice of 2 lemons

60ml extra-virgin olive oil

1 tbsp fresh tarragon, finely chopped

1 tsp turmeric

Seared Scallops

2 tbsp extra-virgin olive oil

2 tbsp salted butter

18 fresh large scallops, shell removed
  and cleaned

Salt & pepper

And finally…

40g chervil

Lemon and Tarragon Oil

Place all the ingredients in a squeezy bottle. Shake it vigorously, then leave to one side.

Seared Scallops

Heat the olive oil and butter together in a medium non-stick pan until it's very hot. Season the scallops with salt & pepper and then add them to the pan. Cook on each side for 2 minutes until they're golden. Remove them from the heat and place them on a plate.

And finally…

Leave the clingfilm on and, using a sharp knife, cut the terrine into six equal slices, as pictured. Lay a slice of terrine on the centre of each of six large plates and then remove the clingfilm.

Take three of the scallops and arrange them evenly around the terrine. Shake the dressing in the squeezy bottle and put about 1 tsp of dressing on each scallop. Place a piece of picked chervil on each of the scallops and serve

Chef's tips

A terrine can be purchased from any high street cookware shop and the wooden block can be bought from a DIY store and cut to fit the top. Tightly wrapping the wooden block in clingfilm will prevent it from spoiling the terrine.

MEAT

The Specialist Schools and Academies Trust has held its national conference at The ICC for the past five years. The quality of catering has been very impressive and delegates comment on the quality of the food and excellent service during the conference dinners. SSAT has worked with the catering staff over the years to develop a range of lunchtime concepts to meet the needs of our delegates and exhibitors. This year the theme of our conference was sustainability and we were delighted that this is also high on The ICC's agenda.

Lyn Simmons
Conference Manager, Specialist Schools and Academies Trust

One-bone Rack of Lamb with Minted Lamb Faggot, Choron Sauce and Butter-fried Baby Vegetables

This dish looks impressive, tastes wonderful and is perfect for a spring dinner party…

Butter Roast Potato

6 medium baking potatoes, peeled
1 tbsp vegetable oil
1 litre vegetable stock (see page 207)
40g salted butter, melted
1 sprig thyme
Salt & pepper

Butter Roast Potato

Pre-heat the oven to 150°C. Using a 5cm stainless steel round cutter (available from any high street cookware shop), cut each potato into a cylinder shape and remove the excess potato from each end. Heat the vegetable oil until hot in a non-stick frying pan, cook one end of each potato until golden brown and place them into a deep roasting tray, browned side up. Bring the vegetable stock to the boil and pour over the potatoes, leaving a 1cm gap from the top of the potato. Add the butter, thyme and salt & pepper and place in the oven for 1 hour until cooked. Remove from the oven and leave in the stock to keep warm.

Minted Lamb Faggot

400g minced lamb
200g pork sausagemeat
30g white breadcrumbs
1 tbsp fresh mint, chopped
1 small onion, peeled and chopped
2 cloves of garlic, peeled
2 tbsp plain flour
1 tbsp vegetable oil

Minted Lamb Faggot

Pre-heat the oven to 160°C. Place the lamb, sausagemeat, breadcrumbs, mint, onion and garlic in a food processor and blitz for 30 seconds until all ingredients are together.

Remove the mixture from the food processor and place in a chilled mixing bowl. Lightly dust the work surface with flour and divide the mixture into six equal pieces. Using the palm of your hands and the floured work surface, roll the mixture into six equal balls.

Pre-heat a medium non-stick ovenproof frying-pan. Add the vegetable oil and gently fry the faggots over a high heat until golden brown all over. Place in the oven, in the pan, for 10-12 minutes until cooked. Remove from the oven and keep them warm.

Choron Sauce

120ml tarragon vinegar

6 peppercorns

25g parsley

2 shallots, finely diced

300g butter

3 egg yolks

Salt & pepper

1 tbsp sun-blushed tomatoes,
  chopped

Sprig of tarragon, chopped

Choron Sauce

Place the vinegar, peppercorns, parsley and shallots in a small saucepan and bring to the boil. Simmer vigorously for 3 minutes, which should reduce the liquid by half. Pour the reduction through a fine sieve into a clean bowl and set aside.

Put the butter in a small saucepan, then place that pan inside a larger pan of simmering water, taking care not to get the butter wet. Wait until the butter has fully melted and then, with a ladle, take out the clear clarified butter, leaving impurities (which will be a whitish colour) in the bottom of the pan. Leave to one side to cool down slightly, but don't allow it to go cold.

Put the egg yolks in a bowl, add the salt & pepper and whisk together. Add the vinegar reduction and whisk until it's mixed together. Put the bowl over a saucepan of simmering water and continually whisk until the mixture starts to thicken and takes on a creamy consistency, then remove from the heat.

Gradually add the clarified butter, whisking all the time until all the butter has been added. This should take 6-7 minutes. Take care not to overheat the mixture or it will split.

Mix the chopped sun-blushed tomatoes and tarragon into the sauce. Cover and leave to one side.

Rack of Lamb

6 x 3-bone racks of lamb, fat and
  two end bones removed
Salt & pepper
1 tbsp vegetable oil
1 tbsp butter

Butter-fried Baby Vegetables

18 baby carrots, sliced in half
12 baby leeks, sliced in half
½ tbsp butter
6 baby courgettes, sliced in half
75g Girolle mushrooms, brushed clean
  and sliced
75g Pied Blue mushrooms, brushed clean
  and sliced

Red Wine Sauce

450ml red wine sauce (see page 209)

Rack of Lamb

Pre-heat the oven to 170°C. Season the lamb liberally with salt & pepper. Place a large non-stick ovenproof frying pan on the stove and heat the olive oil until hot.

Add the lamb and fry over a high heat for 2 minutes until it's golden brown all over. Add the butter, baste the lamb and place in the oven for 10 minutes, if you like it cooked pink. If you prefer it well done, then cook it for 15 minutes.

Remove the lamb from the oven and allow it to rest.

Butter-fried Baby Vegetables

Bring a medium saucepan of salted water to the boil. Cook the carrots for 1 minute. Add the leeks and cook for a further minute, drain and keep warm.

Heat a medium frying pan on the hob and add the butter. Add the courgettes and mushrooms to the pan and sauté for 2 minutes. Add the baby vegetables and sauté for a further minute. Remove from the pan and keep the vegetable mix warm.

Red Wine Sauce

Heat the red wine sauce in a small saucepan.

And finally…

Place one potato to the side of each of six large warm serving plates. Set one faggot to the side of the potato and position the vegetables in front of the potato and faggot. Place the lamb on top of the vegetables with the bone leaning over the faggot. Spoon the Choron sauce over the lamb, the red wine sauce around the faggot and vegetables and serve.

Roast Breast of Duck with a Duck Confit Rosti and Savoury Rhubarb Crumble

Duck is a favourite at dinner parties, but this dish adds another dimension and tastes just as good as it looks…

Duck Confit Rosti

500g duck or goose fat

2 duck legs

2 cloves of garlic

2 sprigs thyme

6 baking potatoes, peeled

Salt & pepper

Duck Confit Rosti

Pre-heat the oven to 140°C. Place a medium ovenproof saucepan on the hob. Add the fat – keeping back 1 tbsp – and heat until it has melted. Season the duck legs with salt & pepper and add them to the fat, along with the garlic and thyme. Bring to the boil, then place in the oven for two hours until the duck is tender. Carefully remove the duck from the fat and allow to cool.

Peel the potatoes and slice them into thin strips using a mandolin with a fine cutter attached. Place them in a bowl, liberally sprinkle with salt and leave for 10 minutes. This will draw out most of the water and make for much easier cooking.

Squeeze out most of the water from the potatoes by hand. Place the potatoes on a clean cloth, wrap it around the potatoes and squeeze the remaining water. Place the potatoes in a clean bowl, add the chopped thyme and season with salt & pepper.

Remove the skin from the duck legs and flake the meat off the bone using your fingers. Add the duck leg confit to the potato and mix thoroughly. Pre-heat six 10cm non-stick tartlet tins in the oven. Add a little goose fat to each tin and return to the oven until the fat is very hot. Divide the potato and duck leg confit mix into six and place into the tartlet tins. Cook them for 5 minutes, until they're golden brown. Turn them over with a palette knife and cook for another 2 minutes. Remove from the tins and keep them warm.

Savoury Rhubarb Crumble

1.1kg fresh rhubarb

1 tbsp caster sugar

1 star anise

1 cinnamon stick

50g melted butter

125g white fresh breadcrumbs

25g Parmesan, freshly grated

1 tsp fresh sage, chopped

1 tsp fresh thyme, chopped

Savoury Rhubarb Crumble

Pre-heat a small saucepan. Cut the red part of the rhubarb into 2.5cm pieces and place in the saucepan with the sugar, star anise, cinnamon stick and 1 tbsp of water. Cook over a medium heat for 30 minutes until the rhubarb is tender and the excess liquid has evaporated. Remove the cinnamon stick and star anise, mix in half the breadcrumbs and allow the mixture to cool. Place the rhubarb in a clean tea towel and gently squeeze to remove any excess liquid.

Pre-heat the oven to 170°C. Brush six 5cm stainless steel rings with melted butter and place them on a baking tray. Fill the rings with the rhubarb mix until they're three-quarters full. Mix the breadcrumbs, Parmesan, sage and thyme and fill the moulds to the top with the crumble mix. Brush with melted butter and place in the oven for 15-20 minutes until golden brown. Remove from the oven and allow them to settle for at least 5 minutes before you remove them from the mould.

Cassis Jus

75g unsalted butter

40g shallots, finely chopped

40g carrots, finely chopped

40g celery, finely chopped

1 clove of garlic, crushed

50ml Cassis

450ml red wine sauce (see page 209)

1 sprig thyme

Salt & pepper

Cassis Jus

Put a little of the butter in a medium pan. Add the vegetables and garlic and cook over a high heat until they are lightly coloured. Add the cassis to the vegetables and reduce by half; this should take around 5 minutes. Then add the red wine sauce and bring back to the boil. Remove from the heat. Add the thyme and leave to infuse in the sauce for 5 minutes, then pass it through a fine sieve. Whisk in the remaining diced butter, a little at a time, to give the sauce a nice sheen.

Duck Breasts

6 x 200g Maigret duck breasts

Salt & pepper

Creamed Green Beans

250ml double cream

200g fine green beans

1 clove of garlic, chopped

Salt & pepper

Vegetable Garnish

18 baby carrots, peeled

100g baby asparagus

1 tbsp butter

50g broad beans, peeled

50g chick peas, tinned

Salt & pepper

Duck Breasts

Pre-heat the oven to 170°C. Heat a large non-stick, ovenproof frying pan. Using a sharp knife, score the skin side of the duck breasts and season liberally. Place the duck breasts, skin side down, into the pan and cook over a high heat for 3 minutes until they're golden brown. Turn them over and cook for a further minute. Remove any excess fat from the pan and place in the oven for 10 minutes (15 minutes for well done). Remove from the oven and allow them to rest.

Creamed Green Beans

Pour the cream into a medium saucepan and heat until boiling. Top and tail the beans. Slice in half and add to the cream, along with the chopped garlic. Bring back to the boil and cook over a high heat for 4-5 minutes until the cream has reduced and the beans are cooked. Season and keep them warm.

Vegetable Garnish

Bring a small pan of salted water to the boil. Add the carrots and cook for 2 minutes, then add the asparagus and cook for a further minute. Place a medium frying pan on the hob and melt the butter. Add the broad beans and chick peas and cook for 1 minute, then add the carrots and asparagus. Toss with the chick peas and beans, season and keep it warm.

And finally…

Place one rosti in the centre of each large warm serving bowl or plate. Place the crumble on the plate next to the rosti and remove the metal ring. Spoon the creamed green beans on top of the rosti and arrange the vegetable garnish around the plate. Slice the duck breast in half lengthways and place on top of the creamed greens. Spoon the sauce around the plate and serve.

Pan-fried Fillets of Beef with Spinach Yorkshire Pudding, Shallot and Garlic Confit and Baby Carrots

This dish offers an elegant take on the classic beef with Yorkshire pudding...

Yorkshire Pudding

150ml vegetable oil

2 large eggs

150g plain flour

300ml milk

100g spinach leaves, torn

25g butter

Salt & pepper

Yorkshire Pudding

Pre-heat the oven to 220°C. Put 1 tbsp of oil into six 10cm Yorkshire pudding tins, then place on a flat tray in the oven.

Crack the eggs into a bowl, add the flour, milk, salt & pepper and whisk until you have a smooth mixture. Pass through a fine sieve into a clean jug.

Pre-heat a medium non-stick frying pan. Add the butter and cook the spinach over a medium heat for a minute or so until wilted. Season with salt & pepper and drain on kitchen roll.

Carefully remove the oiled tins from the oven. Pour the Yorkshire pudding mix into the six tins and place a teaspoon of spinach into the centre of each. Put the tins back in the oven and cook them for 20 minutes until golden brown. Remove from the oven and allow them to cool.

Fondant Potatoes

6 medium baking potatoes, peeled

1 tbsp vegetable oil

1 litre vegetable stock (see page 207)

28g salted butter

Salt & pepper

Fondant Potatoes

Pre-heat the oven to 150°C. Using a 5cm stainless steel round cutter (available from any high street cookware shop), cut each potato into a cylinder shape and remove the excess potato from each end. Heat the vegetable oil in a non-stick frying pan until it is hot, cook one end of each potato until golden brown and place in a deep roasting tray, browned side up.

Bring the vegetable stock to the boil and pour over the potatoes, leaving a 1cm gap from the top of the potatoes. Add the butter and seasoning. Place in the oven for 1 hour until cooked. Remove from the oven and leave in the stock to keep warm.

Confit of Garlic and Shallot

3 large banana shallots

1 tbsp olive oil

Sea salt

6 cloves of garlic

Sprig of thyme

Confit of Garlic and Shallot

Pre-heat oven to 160°C. Place the banana shallots in an ovenproof dish, drizzle with olive oil and sprinkle with sea salt. Cover with tin foil and place in the oven for 45 minutes.

Remove the shallots from the oven, add the garlic and cover again with tin foil. Place back in the oven and cook for a further 30 minutes.

Remove from the oven and allow to cool. Heat a medium non-stick frying pan and add the olive oil. Peel the skin from the shallots and garlic, cut each shallot in half lengthways and place, flat side down, in the frying pan. Cook over a high heat for 2 minutes until the shallots are golden brown. Add the thyme and garlic and cook for a further 30 seconds. Remove from the heat and keep them warm.

Vegetable Garnish

18 baby carrots, peeled

175g green beans

100ml water

½ tbsp butter

1 tsp caster sugar

Salt & pepper

Vegetable Garnish

Heat a medium saucepan, add the carrots, water, butter, sugar and salt & pepper and cook over a medium heat for 3-4 minutes with the lid on. Remove the lid and cook for a further 2 minutes; this will reduce the cooking liquor and ensure the carrots become glazed. Remove from the heat and keep warm.

Bring a small pan of salted water to the boil, add the green beans and cook for a minute or so until they are tender. Drain the beans into a colander, mix with the carrots and keep them warm.

Pan-fried Beef Fillets

½ tbsp olive oil

12 x 80g beef fillet medallions

Salt & pepper

½ tbsp butter

Red Wine Sauce

450ml red wine sauce (see page 209)

Pan-fried Beef Fillets

Heat the olive oil in a large, non-stick frying pan on the hob. Season the beef with salt & pepper and pan-fry them over a high heat for 1 minute each side until golden brown on both sides and cooked rare. Add the knob of butter and baste the beef. Cook for 1-2 minutes each side for rare or 3-4 minutes each side for well done. Remove from the heat and keep warm.

Red Wine Sauce

Heat the red wine sauce in a small saucepan.

And finally…

Place one fondant potato on each of the six large, warmed serving plates. Set the baby carrots and green beans alongside the potato. Place one fillet of beef on top of the other. Slightly warm the Yorkshire puddings under the grill and place next to the fillets, as pictured. Stack the shallots and garlic confit on top of the fillet steaks, spoon the sauce over and around the dish and serve.

Braised Blade of Beef and Italian Meatballs with Grilled Polenta

This is a hearty, warming dish, which is elegant and delicious…

Braised Blade of Beef

2 tbsp olive oil

125g plain flour

Salt & pepper

6 x 175g blades of beef

2 carrots, peeled

1 white onion, peeled

2 celery sticks

Sprig of thyme

2 cloves of garlic, chopped

2 tbsp tomato purée

200ml red wine

1.5 litre brown chicken stock
  (see page 208)

40g cold unsalted butter, diced

Braised Blade of Beef

Pre-heat the oven to 160°C. Heat 1 tbsp of olive oil in a large ovenproof casserole on the hob. Pour the flour on to a plate and season it with salt & pepper. Place the blades of beef in the flour until they're coated on both sides. Shake any excess flour back on to the plate – keeping it aside for later – and place them in the casserole. Cook them for 3 minutes on each side until they are golden brown and then remove them from the casserole.

Do not clean the casserole. Roughly chop the carrots, onion and celery. Place the casserole back on the hob and heat another tbsp of olive oil. Add the chopped vegetables, thyme and garlic. Cook for 5 minutes until the vegetables are golden brown all over, then add 55g of the seasoned flour and stir in well. Add the tomato purée, red wine and chicken stock and bring to the boil.

Remove from the heat and add the beef to the casserole and cover with a lid. Place in the pre-heated oven for around 1½ hours until the beef is tender.

Remove the blades of beef from the liquor and keep them warm. Put the casserole back on the hob and bring the liquor to the boil and reduce it by a third. Remove from the heat and pass it through a fine sieve into another saucepan. If the sauce is the correct consistency it should coat the back of a stainless steel spoon, if it is too thick add a little water. Season with salt & pepper to taste, then whisk in the diced butter a little at a time. This will give the sauce a nice sheen. Ensure it stays warm.

Italian Meatballs

2 tbsp olive oil

1 white onion, peeled

2 cloves of garlic

750g minced lean beef

300g pork sausagemeat

50g white breadcrumbs

75g Parmesan, freshly grated

1 free-range egg

1 tbsp parsley, chopped

1 tbsp Worcestershire sauce

1 tsp English mustard powder

Salt & pepper

Grilled Polenta

750ml of vegetable stock
 (see page 207)

85g butter

200g medium polenta

75g Parmesan, freshly grated

½ tbsp chives, chopped

½ tbsp tarragon, chopped

Salt & pepper

1 tbsp olive oil

Italian Meatballs

Pre-heat the oven to 160°C. Heat 1 tbsp of the olive oil in a non-stick frying pan. Finely dice the onion and garlic and gently cook them for 3 minutes. Remove them from the heat and allow them to cool. Place the onion, garlic and the rest of the ingredients in a large bowl and mix until all the ingredients are blended together.

Roll the mix into 12 equal balls and place them in the fridge for a couple of hours. Heat the remaining olive oil in a non-stick frying pan. Place the meatballs in the pan. Keep gently shaking the pan to avoid the meatballs overcooking in any one place – they need to be evenly browned. Remove from the pan and place the meatballs onto a baking tray. Cook for 15-20 minutes in the pre-heated oven. Remove them from the oven and keep them warm.

Grilled Polenta

Pour the stock into a large pot and put it on the hob. Add the butter and simmer gently. Gradually add the polenta, whisking thoroughly and cook for 30 minutes. Remove it from the heat and stir in the Parmesan, chives, tarragon and salt & pepper. Place a piece of greaseproof paper into a 5cm deep tray. Pour in the polenta mix and make it level with a palette knife. Leave to one side, uncovered until it's cool enough to cut. Remove the polenta from the tray on to a chopping board. Slice into six rectangular pieces roughly 4cm by 8cm. Pre-heat a grill-pan on the hob until it's very hot.

Brush the top of the polenta with the olive oil and place it in the grill-pan. Cook for 1 minute then, lifting it with the palette knife, turn it 45° and place it back on the stove for another minute. This will give the polenta a char-grilled appearance. Transfer to a plate until it is needed and keep it warm.

Vegetable Garnish

4 medium carrots, peeled
1 celeriac, peeled
350g wild mushrooms, brushed clean
1 tbsp olive oil
25g butter
6 asparagus spears
Salt & pepper

Vegetable Garnish

Cut the carrots and celeriac into approximately 2.5cm pieces. Bring a medium saucepan of water to the boil and add the carrots. Cook for 2 minutes. Add the celeriac and cook for another 3 minutes. Remove from the pan and cool rapidly in very cold water.

Cut the mushrooms into 2.5cm pieces. Heat the olive oil and butter in a large non-stick frying pan on the hob, add the carrot, celeriac and cook for 3 minutes until they are lightly coloured. Add the mushrooms to the pan and cook for a further 3 minutes until the garnish is a light golden brown. Season with salt & pepper and remove from the pan and keep them warm.

Cut the asparagus into 12cm lengths and lightly peel 2cm from the bottom. Bring a medium pot of salted water to the boil, add the asparagus and cook for 2 minutes. Remove from the water and keep them warm.

And finally…

Place one piece of polenta on each of six large warm serving plates. Place two of the meatballs to the side of the polenta and position the vegetable garnish between the polenta and the meatballs. Lay the blade of beef on top of the meatballs and vegetable garnish and set the asparagus on top of the beef. Spoon the sauce over and around the beef.

Paprika-roasted Breast of Chicken with Creamed Greens and Smoked Bacon, Rosti Potatoes and Tarragon Sauce

Chicken and tarragon work well together, but the spice of the paprika adds a surprising note to this dish…

Rosti Potatoes

6 large baking potatoes
1 sprig thyme, picked and roughly chopped
Salt & pepper
6 tbsp olive oil

Rosti Potatoes

Peel the potatoes and slice them into thin strips using a mandolin with a fine cutter attached. Place them in a bowl and liberally sprinkle with salt. This will draw out most of the water and make for easier cooking.

By hand, squeeze out most of the water from the potatoes. Place the potatoes on a clean cloth, wrap it around the potatoes and squeeze the remaining water. Place the potatoes in a clean bowl, add the chopped thyme and season with salt & pepper.

Pre-heat the oven to 160°C. Drizzle olive oil into six 10cm non-stick tartlet tins and heat them in the oven for a few minutes. Divide the potato into six and place it in the tins; gently cook for 10 minutes until golden brown, turn them over and cook for another 10 minutes until golden brown on both sides. Remove from the tins and keep the rostis warm.

Paprika Chicken

6 x 280g corn-fed chicken breast, skin
  and bone on (ask the butcher to
  French trim the bone)
6 wooden skewers
2 tbsp butter
1 tbsp paprika
Salt & pepper

Paprika Chicken

Pre-heat the oven to 170°C. Take each chicken breast and fold it in half lengthways to resemble a circle, as pictured. Skewer the chicken to hold the shape. Melt the butter in a small saucepan and add the paprika. Brush the chicken liberally with the butter and paprika mix. Season with salt & pepper and place in the oven for 18-20 minutes until golden brown and cooked through. Remove from the oven and keep the chicken warm.

Creamed Cabbage and Smoked Bacon

2 cloves of garlic, peeled
400ml cream
1 sprig thyme
450g spring cabbage
6 slices rindless smoked bacon

Vegetable Garnish

500g small Chantenay carrots, scrubbed
12 baby asparagus spears
200g wild mushrooms, brushed clean
100g Girolle mushrooms, brushed clean
1 tbsp olive oil
1 tbsp butter
Salt & pepper

Tarragon Sauce

450ml red wine sauce (see page 209)
1 sprig tarragon
40g cold butter, diced

Creamed Cabbage and Smoked Bacon

Crush the garlic with a rolling pin. Pour the cream into a medium saucepan. Put the crushed garlic and sprig of thyme in the cream, bring to the boil and then simmer for 20 minutes. Remove from the heat, then pass through a fine strainer and keep the cream warm.

Wash the cabbage, remove the thick stems and slice it finely. Bring a medium pan of water to the boil and cook the cabbage for 4 minutes. Drain through a colander and put into very cold water to prevent it from over-cooking. Drain and squeeze the excess water from the cabbage and set to one side. Grill the bacon for about 3 minutes on each side, until cooked. Set aside and keep it warm.

Vegetable Garnish

Bring a large pan of salted water to the boil and cook the carrots for 4 minutes. Remove from the heat, drain and keep them warm. Place the pan of water back on the stove, bring to the boil and add the asparagus. Cook for 1 minute, remove from the heat, drain and keep warm with the carrots. Thickly slice the mushrooms. Heat a large non-stick frying pan and add the olive oil and butter. Sauté the mushrooms for 2-3 minutes, then remove from the heat, season with salt & pepper and keep them warm.

Tarragon Sauce

Heat the red wine sauce, add the tarragon and leave to infuse for 5 minutes. Remove from the heat, pass through a fine sieve and then whisk in the cold diced butter, a little at a time, to give the sauce a nice sheen.

And finally…

Heat a non-stick frying pan on the stove and gently heat the cream. Add the cabbage and cook for 2 minutes until hot. Season and keep hot. Place the rostis at the centre of each of six large warm serving plates. Divide the cabbage into six equal portions, place on top of the rostis, with two spears of baby asparagus. Fold the bacon and place on top of the cabbage.

Gently remove the skewer from the chicken and lay the chicken on top of the bacon. Set four of the Chantenay carrots around the chicken and place the mushrooms around the carrots. Spoon the sauce around the carrots and over the chicken and serve.

Warm char-grilled Lemon Chicken Salad with over-baked Parma Ham and Caesar Dressing

Classic ingredients are given a fresh twist with this new take on lemon chicken…

Crisp Parma Ham

6 slices Parma ham

Crisp Parma Ham

Place a piece of greaseproof paper on a baking sheet. Lay slices of the Parma ham in a row on the paper, ensuring none overlaps. Place another piece of greaseproof paper on top of the ham and another baking sheet on top to weigh it down; this ensures the ham stays flat.

Pre-heat the oven to 160°C. Place the trays in the oven and cook for around 20 minutes. Remove from the oven and allow to cool with the trays and paper still in place. Gently remove the Parma ham, put on a plate and set aside.

Lemon Chicken

2 tbsp extra-virgin olive oil
2 cloves of garlic, crushed
1 large lemon
1 sprig tarragon, chopped
1 tsp turmeric powder
6 x 225g skinless chicken breasts
Salt & pepper

Lemon Chicken

Pre-heat the oven to 160°C. Trim off any excess fat from the chicken breast, place in a bowl with olive oil and garlic. Squeeze over the lemon juice and chop the remaining lemon and add it to the bowl along with the tarragon and turmeric. Turn over the chicken in the marinade, mix well and leave to marinate for at least 4 hours in the fridge (preferably overnight).

Heat a grill-pan on the hob. Remove the chicken breasts from the marinade, season with salt & pepper and place in the grill pan. Cook for 2 minutes, then lift each piece of chicken and turn it 45° and place it back in the pan, same side down, to obtain a "criss-cross" pattern. Cook for a further 2 minutes, until they appear char-grilled. Remove from the char-grill and place on a baking tray. Cook in the oven for 15 minutes, then remove from oven and allow to cool.

Vermicelli Noodles

1 litre vegetable stock (see page 207)
350g vermicelli noodles
1 tbsp fresh coriander, chopped

Vermicelli Noodles

Pour the stock into a medium saucepan and bring to the boil. Remove from the heat and drop in the noodles. Leave for 5 minutes or until the noodles are soft. Drain the noodles and put them under cold running water until they're cold. Place in a bowl with chopped coriander and put them in the fridge until they're needed.

Focaccia Croute

1 medium focaccia loaf
1 tbsp extra-virgin olive oil
1 tbsp dried mixed herbs
Sea salt
Cracked black pepper

Focaccia Croute

Pre-heat the oven to 160°C. Cut the focaccia into six thin slices and lay them on greaseproof paper on a baking sheet. Drizzle with olive oil and sprinkle with the mixed herbs, sea salt and cracked black pepper. Bake in the oven for 10 minutes until golden brown. Allow to cool.

Salad

12 red cherry tomatoes
1 tbsp olive oil
1 red pepper, cut into 12
1 yellow pepper, cut into 12
150g pitted black olives
18 sun-blushed tomatoes
6 little gem
180g mizuna

Caesar Dressing

20g anchovy fillets
½ clove of garlic, peeled
3 tbsp Parmesan, freshly grated
200ml olive oil
Juice of ½ lemon

Salad

Heat a non-stick frying-pan. Cut the cherry tomatoes in half and place them, flat side down, in the pan for 20 seconds until blackened. Remove from the heat and place in the fridge to chill. Heat the olive oil in the same pan and cook the peppers until they are lightly coloured. Remove from the pan and allow them to cool. Slice the olives in half and add to the peppers, then add the sun-blushed tomatoes. Pick off the outer leaves from the little gem lettuces and discard. Cut each lettuce into four, wash off any dirt and drain on kitchen roll. Wash the mizuna leaves and again drain on kitchen roll.

Caesar Dressing

Place all the ingredients in a blender and blitz until thick and creamy. Remove from the blender, transfer to a squeezy bottle and place in the fridge until needed.

And finally…

Divide the noodles between six large serving bowls or plates. Place the mizuna leaf on top of the noodles and place four quarters of the little gem lettuce evenly around the side of the bowl.

Set the peppers, tomatoes and olives around the noodles. Lay half a piece of the dried Parma ham on top of the mizuna. Slice the chicken in half lengthways and put one half of the chicken on the Parma ham. Lay the other half of the Parma ham on top of the chicken and the final piece of chicken on top.

Lay the focaccia croute on top of the chicken, squeeze the Caesar dressing around the salad, over the chicken and serve.

Chump of Lamb with Mozzarella Ciabatta Mash and Balsamic Cherry Tomatoes

Balsamic vinegar complements the lamb perfectly and creates a dish full of interesting flavours and textures…

Chump of Lamb

6 x 250g chump/rump of lamb
2 tbsp olive oil
Salt & pepper

Chump of Lamb

Pre-heat the oven to 170°C. Score the skin of the lamb in a criss-cross fashion, taking care not to cut too deep.

Heat the olive oil in an ovenproof, non-stick frying pan. Season the lamb and cook it skin side down for 2-3 minutes, then turn it over and repeat the process.

Place the pan in the pre-heated oven and cook for 15-18 minutes. Transfer the lamb to a clean plate and allow it to rest for 5 minutes.

Mozzarella Ciabatta Mash

½ small ciabatta loaf
900g Maris Piper potatoes, peeled
  and quartered
100g unsalted butter
120ml double cream
Salt & pepper
Nutmeg, freshly grated
175g mozzarella, grated

Mozzarella Ciabatta Mash

Pre-heat the oven to 170°C. Slice the ciabatta thinly, place on a baking sheet and cook in the oven until crisp and lightly golden; this should take around 5 minutes. Remove from the oven and allow to cool before roughly breaking up into small pieces.

Boil the potatoes in salted water for about 20 minutes until soft. Drain and put back into the saucepan. Cover with a lid and shake the pan vigorously to break up the potatoes. Add the butter and cream while mashing the potatoes. Season with salt & pepper and mix in the nutmeg.

Transfer to a small roasting tin. Top with roughly crushed ciabatta and liberally cover with grated mozzarella. Put in the oven at 160°C for 10 minutes or until the topping becomes golden brown.

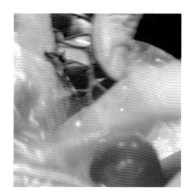

Cherry Tomatoes and Green Beans

1 red pepper

1 yellow pepper

200g fine green beans

150g red cherry tomatoes

150g yellow cherry tomatoes

2 tbsp extra-virgin olive oil

1 tbsp balsamic vinegar

1 tbsp Demerara sugar

Salt & pepper

Red Wine Sauce

450ml red wine sauce (see page 209)

Cherry Tomatoes and Green Beans

De-seed the peppers and thinly slice. Top and tail the beans, drop them into boiling water and cook for 2 minutes. Drain and then put into ice water to maintain their colour. Cut all the tomatoes in half and set aside. Heat the olive oil in a medium, non-stick frying pan until it's very hot. Add the peppers and stir-fry for a few seconds before adding the tomatoes, green beans, balsamic vinegar and sugar. Cook until the vegetables become lightly caramelised; this should take 3-4 minutes. Season to taste.

Red Wine Sauce

Heat the red wine sauce in a small saucepan.

And finally…

Take six large serving plates and put a large spoon of ciabatta mash to one side of each. Slice each piece of lamb twice to give three good-sized pieces. Set along side the mash and then arrange the cherry tomatoes and green beans next to the lamb. Pour a little sauce over the lamb and vegetables.

Veal Saltimbocca with Potato, Parmesan and Spinach Fritter and Shiraz Sauce

A contemporary take on a classic dish, this recipe can work just as well with chicken in place of veal...

Veal Escalope

6 x 175g veal escalopes

1 sprig sage

12 Parma ham slices

1 tbsp olive oil

Salt & pepper

Veal Escalope

Lay out approx 60cm of clingfilm on a work surface. Place the veal escalopes on top and then lay two 60cm of clingfilm on top of the veal. Using a meat bat or rolling pin, bat out the veal until it becomes 3-4mm thick and is roughly 12cm square.

Cut the six squares in half so you have 12 rectangular veal escalopes. Place one sage leaf on to one side of the veal and fold in half. Lay one piece of Parma ham on a work surface, then place the veal to one end and wrap the ham around the veal.

Place a large non-stick frying pan on the stove and add the olive oil. Season the veal and place in the pan. Cook for 4 minutes until they're golden brown. Turn them over and repeat the process. Remove from the pan and keep them warm.

Potato, Parmesan and Spinach Fritter

40g butter

150g fresh spinach leaves

300g Desirée potatoes, peeled and
  chopped

300ml water

125g butter

125g plain flour

4 whole eggs

1 tsp olive oil

Salt & pepper

Potato, Parmesan and Spinach Fritter

Pre-heat a medium non-stick frying pan, add the butter and cook the spinach over a medium heat for 1 minute until it's wilted. Season with salt & pepper and drain on kitchen roll. Coarsely chop the spinach and chill it until it's needed.

Bring a medium pan of salted water to the boil, add the potatoes and cook for 20 minutes. Drain through a colander and then put back in same saucepan over the heat. Shake the pan and mix with a wooden spoon vigorously to break up the potatoes. Remove them from the heat, mash the potatoes until there are no lumps. Place them in a bowl and refrigerate.

Put the water and butter in a medium saucepan and bring to the boil. Add the flour and beat for 2 minutes over the heat until you have a smooth paste. Remove from the heat, place in a mixing bowl. Gradually add the eggs, a little at a time, until they are all added, mixing all the time. This is a basic choux paste mix and will form the base of the potatoes. Allow to cool then refrigerate for 1 hour.

Remove the choux paste from the fridge and add the mashed potato, spinach and salt & pepper. Mix all the ingredients together and leave to one side.

Pre-heat a deep-fat fryer to 165°C. Brush a tablespoon with olive oil. Scoop out a tablespoon of the potato fritter mix and, using another tablespoon to scrape it off, gently place it in the fryer. Cook evenly for 2-3 minutes until golden brown. Remove from the oil, drain on kitchen roll and keep it warm. Repeat until you have used all the mixture.

Vegetable Garnish

150g green beans

150g sugar snap peas

6 asparagus spears

2 red peppers, de-seeded

2 yellow peppers, de-seeded

1 tbsp olive oil

Shiraz Sauce

450ml red wine sauce (see page 209)

For Shiraz wine sauce simply substitute the red wine for Shiraz wine

Vegetable Garnish

Bring a small pan of salted water to the boil, add the green beans and sugar snap peas and cook for 1 minute until they're tender. Remove them from the water and keep them warm. Bring the pan of water back to the boil and add the asparagus, cook for 2-3 minutes, then remove from the water and keep warm.

Cut the peppers to roughly the same size as the sugar snap peas. Heat a large, non-stick frying pan on the hob. Heat the olive oil and add the peppers, then cook on a high heat for 3 minutes until they're lightly golden. Remove from the heat and keep them warm. Mix the vegetable garnish together, apart from the asparagus spears, and keep warm.

Shiraz Sauce

Heat the Shiraz sauce in a small saucepan.

And finally…

Divide the vegetable garnish into six and place a pile to one side of each of six large, warm plates. Lay two of the veal escalopes on the edge of the vegetables as pictured. Lean one of the potato fritters on the veal and lay a piece of asparagus on top of the veal. Spoon the sauce on top of the veal and around the vegetables and serve.

Pan-fried Venison Cutlets with Port Wine Cabbage, Lavender Anna Potatoes and Blueberry and Balsamic Jus

A fantastic combination of colour and flavour, this dish is sure to get people talking...

Lavender Anna Potatoes

1.5kg Maris Piper potatoes, peeled
Salt & pepper
¼ tsp fresh lavender, finely chopped
200g melted butter

Lavender Anna Potatoes

Pre-heat the oven to 160°C. Slice the potatoes thinly and evenly. Place in a colander and liberally sprinkle with salt & pepper, then leave to one side for 5 minutes to drain any excess water.

Remove from the colander and dry off on kitchen roll. Sprinkle the lavender over the potatoes. Layer the potatoes neatly in six 10cm tartlet tins until the mould is well filled. The first layer in the tin will be the presentation side so make sure you arrange it as neatly as possible. Pour the butter equally over the top of the potatoes, place in the oven and cook for 40-45 minutes until golden brown. Remove from the oven and keep warm.

Port Wine Cabbage

1 medium red cabbage
3 red apples
150ml redcurrant jelly
150g Demerara sugar
1 cinnamon stick, broken in half
150ml Port wine

Port Wine Cabbage

Pre-heat the oven to 120°C. Peel off the top leaves of the cabbage and discard them. Cut the cabbage into quarters, then remove the core and slice thinly. Remove the core from the apple and cut into small dice. Place the cabbage, apple and remaining ingredients into a suitably sized ovenproof container with a tight-fitting lid and cook in the oven for 1 hour, stirring every 15 minutes. Remove from the oven. Drain into a colander, catching the liquor in a saucepan. Bring the liquid to the boil and reduce by half, then add the cabbage back to the liquor and keep warm.

Blueberry and Balsamic Jus

80g unsalted butter, cold and diced

40g shallots, finely chopped

40g carrots, finely chopped

40g celery, finely chopped

1 clove of garlic, finely chopped

4 tbsp balsamic vinegar

600ml red wine sauce (see page 209)

1 sprig thyme

75g blueberries, washed

Salt & pepper

Red Wine Shallots

3 large banana shallots, peeled

200ml red wine

½ tbsp redcurrant jelly

2 tbsp cassis

1 sprig thyme

1 bay leaf

Blueberry and Balsamic Jus

Take a medium pan and add a little of the butter. Add the vegetables and garlic and cook over a high heat until they're lightly coloured. Add the balsamic vinegar and reduce by half. Add the red wine sauce and reduce by a third; this should take 10 minutes.

Add the thyme and leave to infuse in the sauce for 5 minutes. Remove from the heat and then pass through a fine sieve. Whisk in the remaining diced butter a little at a time to give the sauce a nice sheen. Add the blueberries and season to taste with salt & pepper. Keep the sauce warm until needed.

Red Wine Shallots

Put all the ingredients in a small saucepan and bring to the boil. Simmer for 15-20 minutes until the shallots are soft. Remove the shallots from the pan and slice them in half. Keep them warm until they're needed.

Pan-fried Venison Cutlets

12 x 125g venison cutlets

Salt & pepper

1 tbsp olive oil

1 tbsp butter

Vegetable Garnish

3 large carrots, peeled

75g green beans

50g broad beans

Pan-fried Venison Cutlets

Pre-heat the oven to 170°C. Season the venison with salt & pepper. Heat the olive oil in a large non-stick ovenproof frying pan. Fry the venison over a high heat for 2 minutes until golden brown all over. Place in the oven for 5 minutes until cooked pink (10 minutes for well done). Remove from the oven and allow to rest for 5 minutes.

Vegetable Garnish

Using a small melon baller, cut out 30 small carrot balls and set to one side. Top and tail the green beans and pod the broad beans. Bring a small pan of salted water to the boil. Add the carrots and cook for 3 minutes. Add the green and broad beans and cook for a further 2 minutes. Drain and keep the vegetables hot.

And finally…

Place one of the potato cakes on each of six large warm serving plates. Put a pile of the red cabbage on top. Lean two of the venison cutlets on the side of the red cabbage and lay the red wine shallots between the cutlets. Set the vegetable garnish around the venison, spoon the sauce around the vegetables and serve.

Satay of Chicken, Beef and Pork with Sticky Rice and Thai Stir-fry Vegetables

The eastern fusion of fragrant flavours is sure to make this a huge success...

Mixed Meat Satay

3 x 240g chicken breasts, cut into 2cm dice

360g beef fillet, cut into 2cm dice

360g pork loin, cut into 2cm dice

3 tbsp Thai fish sauce (Nam Pla)

1 tbsp soy sauce

1 sprig coriander

20g ginger, crushed

2 cloves of garlic, crushed

1 red chilli, de-seeded and chopped

You will also need

18 x 6-inch wooden skewers soaked in
 water for 2 hours

Satay Sauce

2 tsp peanut oil

1 white onion, finely chopped

2 cloves of garlic, finely chopped

120g peanut butter

½ tsp Cayenne pepper

600ml water

100g coconut milk

2 tbsp dark soy sauce

Mixed Meat Satay

Thread the diced chicken on to six wooden skewers. Repeat the process with the beef and the pork until you have six of each skewers.

In a large bowl, place the fish sauce, soy sauce, coriander, crushed ginger, crushed garlic and the red chilli. Place the meat satay in the bowl and marinade for 2-3 hours in the fridge.

Satay Sauce

Heat the peanut oil in a medium saucepan, add the onion and garlic and cook for 2 minutes until it's soft. Stir in the peanut butter, Cayenne pepper, half the water and the coconut milk and simmer for 5 minutes. Stir in the soy sauce. If the sauce is too thick, add a little bit of the remaining water to thin it down. Remove from the heat and keep warm.

Sticky Rice Balls

200ml coconut milk

400g jasmine rice

Salt & pepper

20g sesame seeds

Thai Stir-fried Vegetables

2 tbsp peanut oil

20g ginger, freshly grated

2 cloves of garlic, peeled and chopped

1 large carrot, thinly sliced

150g baby sweetcorn, cut in half lengthways

1 red pepper, roughly chopped

1 yellow pepper, roughly chopped

100g beansprouts

1 purple onion, sliced

10 spring onions, chopped

100g fine green beans, topped, tailed and
 cut in half

1 large bok choi, shredded

100g beech mushrooms, brushed clean

100g sugar snap peas

3 tbsp Thai fish sauce (Nam Pla)

2 tbsp soy sauce

1 sprig coriander, chopped

Sticky Rice Balls

Pre-heat a deep-fat fryer to 175°C. Place a medium saucepan of salted water on the stove. Add the coconut milk and bring to the boil. Add the rice and simmer for 12 minutes. Drain the rice through a sieve and place on a baking tray. Season with salt & pepper.

Allow to cool and place in the fridge for 10 minutes. Remove from the fridge and make it into 12 balls by rolling in the palm of your hand. Roll the rice balls in the sesame seeds. Place the rice balls in the fryer and cook for 4-5 minutes until they're golden brown. Remove from the fryer, drain on kitchen roll and keep them warm. You can, of course, shallow fry the rice balls, but it's difficult to achieve such an even colour this way.

Thai Stir-fried Vegetables

Heat the peanut oil in a large wok until it's smoking. Add the ginger and garlic and cook for 30 seconds. Add the carrots, sweetcorn and peppers and cook for 1 minute. Add the rest of the vegetables and mushrooms and cook for another 2 minutes. Put in the fish sauce, soy sauce and coriander and cook for a further 2 minutes. Remove from the pan and keep the vegetables warm.

And finally…

Pre-heat a grill-pan on a high heat. Scrape off the marinade from the meat satay and cook them in the grill-pan for 3 minutes on each of the four sides. Remove from the heat and keep them warm. Divide the stir-fried vegetables between six small, warm serving bowls. Set three satay skewers to the edge of six large serving plates with two rice balls next to them. Spoon the satay sauce and some chopped corriander over the skewers.

Quince-glazed Pork Belly with Cassoulet of Beans and Chilli-roasted Sweet Potato

Pork is the unsung hero of the dinner party – this dish should help put it firmly back on the menu...

Quince-glazed Pork Belly

6 cloves of garlic, peeled

1 bunch sage

2kg boneless pork belly, rind removed

600ml of warm water

1 tbsp olive oil

Salt & pepper

100g plum sauce

150g quince jelly

Quince-glazed Pork Belly

Pre-heat the oven to 140°C. Chop the garlic into small chunks and pick off the sage leaves. Lay the pork belly on a chopping board and cut 2cm incisions, 2cm apart, into the skin side. You should end up with roughly 20 incisions.

Take about half a sage leaf, wrap it around a chunk of garlic and push it into the incision in the pork. Repeat this until you have filled all the holes. Put the pork on a wire rack and place in a large, deep-sided roasting tin and pour the warm water into the bottom of the tin. Drizzle the pork with olive oil and season liberally with salt & pepper. Cover completely with silver foil and place in the oven. Slow cook for 2 hours without removing the foil.

Melt the plum sauce and the quince jelly over a medium heat and pour it over the top of the pork. Place the pork back in the oven and cook for a further 30 minutes until it's golden, glazed and breaks under light pressure. Remove from the oven. Let it rest for 30 minutes covered in foil and keep it warm (it's vitally important to do this as the meat will settle and you'll get a far cleaner cut).

Red Cabbage

1 medium red cabbage

3 red apples

150ml redcurrant jelly

150g Demerara sugar

1 cinnamon stick, broken in half

150ml Port wine

Red Cabbage

Pre-heat the oven to 140°C. Peel off the top leaves of the cabbage and discard them. Cut the cabbage into quarters, remove the core and slice thinly. Remove the cores from the apples and cut them into small dice. Place all of the ingredients into a suitably sized ovenproof container with a tight-fitting lid and cook in the oven for 1 hour, stirring every 15 minutes.

Remove the cabbage from the oven then drain into a colander, catching the liquor in a saucepan. Bring the liquid to the boil and reduce by half, then add the cabbage back to the liquor and keep warm.

Chilli-roasted Sweet Potato

2 medium sweet potatoes
2 tbsp clear honey
1 red chilli, de-seeded and finely chopped
Salt & pepper
25g fresh chopped coriander

Cassoulet of Beans

100g Borlotti beans, tinned
100g broad beans, fresh
100g Cannellini beans, tinned
1 tbsp olive oil
100g pancetta, cubed
Salt & pepper

And finally...

450ml red wine sauce, hot (see page 209)

Chilli-roasted Sweet Potato

Pre-heat the oven to 170°C. Wash the sweet potatoes thoroughly and cut lengthways into three equal wedges. Place them on a medium baking tray. Brush liberally with the honey all over. Sprinkle over the chillies. Season with salt & pepper and place in the oven for 15-20 minutes. Remove from the oven and roll the sweet potatoes in the tray to gather up any remaining honey mix, then sprinkle with the fresh coriander and keep warm.

Cassoulet of Beans

Place the Borlotti and Cannellini beans in a colander and wash them thoroughly. Drain well, place on kitchen roll and set to one side. Place the broad beans in boiling salted water and cook for 2 minutes, then drain into a colander and refresh in cold water.

Peel the broad beans and add to the other beans. Remove the skin from the pancetta and cut into 1cm cubes. Place a medium non-stick frying pan on the hob and add the olive oil. Cook the pancetta for 3 minutes until lightly browned, then add all the beans and cook for a further minute. Season the cassoulet with salt & pepper and keep it warm.

And finally...

Heat the red wine sauce in a small saucepan. Place the pork on a chopping board and slice it into six equal squares. Place a piece of pork to one edge of six large, warm serving plates, as the picture shows. Position a large spoon of the cabbage next to the pork and lean the sweet potato up between the pork and the cabbage. Place the cassoulet of beans to the side of the red cabbage, spoon the sauce around the dish and serve.

Thai slow-cooked Shank of Lamb with Creamed Coconut & Chilli Sauce

This is a fragrant dish, perfect for a long lazy dinner party…

Thai slow-cooked Shank of Lamb

1 tbsp vegetable oil

6 x 450g lamb shanks

1 tbsp green Thai curry paste

1 stick lemongrass, chopped

1 green chilli, chopped

1 star anise

1 cinnamon stick

2 Kaffir lime leaves

2 litres brown chicken stock, warm
  (see page 208)

Thai slow-cooked Shank of Lamb

Pre-heat the oven to 170°C. Heat the vegetable oil in a large ovenproof saucepan. Add the lamb shanks and make sure they are cooked until they're golden brown all over. Remove from the saucepan and place on a tray.

Return the saucepan to the heat, add the curry paste, lemongrass, green chilli, star anise, cinnamon stick and cafier lime leaves and cook for 2 minutes, stirring continuously. Add the chicken stock and bring to the boil, then return the lamb to the saucepan. Place a tight-fitting lid on the saucepan and place in the oven for 2½ hours until the lamb is tender. Once it's cooked, remove it from the oven and keep it warm.

Basmati and Red Camargue Rice

60g Camargue rice

150g wild & basmati rice

150g long grain rice

1 tbsp turmeric

25g butter

Basmati and Red Camargue Rice

Bring a small pan of salted water to the boil. Add the Camargue rice and simmer and for 20-25 minutes. Remove from the heat and strain the rice through a colander and keep it warm.

Cook the wild and basmati rice for 12-15 minutes in a pan of salted water. Drain the rice through a colander and keep it warm.

Bring a small saucepan of salted water to the boil, add the turmeric and the long-grain rice and cook for 15 minutes. Remove from the heat, strain the rice through a colander and keep it warm. Mix the three rices together, in a container, add the butter, stir well and keep warm until needed.

Creamed Coconut and Chilli Sauce

½ tbsp vegetable oil

1 stick lemongrass, chopped

1 red chilli, chopped

1 star anise

450ml red wine sauce (see page 209)

120ml coconut milk

Juice of 1 lime

1 tbsp coriander, chopped

Salt & pepper

Bok Choi and Oriental Mushrooms

½ tbsp vegetable oil

2 medium carrots, peeled and sliced thinly

1 red pepper, de-seeded and diced

3 baby bok choi, sliced in half

150g shiitake mushrooms, brushed clean and sliced

1 packet fresh baby corn, cut in half

Salt & pepper

Creamed Coconut and Chilli Sauce

Heat a small saucepan. Add the vegetable oil, lemongrass, chilli and star anise and cook over a medium heat for 1 minute. Add the red wine sauce and coconut milk and bring to the boil, before simmering for 10 minutes. Pass the sauce through a fine strainer into a clean saucepan, then add the lime juice and chopped coriander, season to taste and keep warm.

Bok Choi and Oriental Mushrooms

Place a wok on a high heat. Add the vegetable oil. Stir-fry the carrot and pepper for 1 minute. Add the mushrooms, baby corn and the bok choi and stir-fry over a high heat. Add 2 tablespoons of water to help steam the vegetables and cook for a further 2 minutes. Remove from the wok, season and keep the vegetables hot.

And finally…

Place a pile of vegetables on to six large, warm serving plates or bowls. Place the rice next to the vegetables and set the lamb shank on top. Spoon the sauce over and around the lamb and serve.

I've been fortunate enough to have attended numerous events in my time and the executive dining experience that accompanies them is often no more than average. However, the culinary offerings served at The NEC during Horse of the Year Show were as beautifully presented as the event itself and were by far the best I have experienced at any venue of its kind.

Gary Stevens
ex-Tottenham and England international footballer

Lime and Coriander Salmon with Udon Noodles, Lotus Root and Chilli Jam

A surprisingly easy dish with a distinctly eastern flavour...

Chilli Jam

5 red chillies, de-seeded and chopped
2 cloves of garlic, chopped
1 tsp fresh ginger, chopped
100g brown sugar
1 tbsp white wine vinegar
60ml clear honey
250ml water
½ lime, juiced

Lime and Coriander Marinade

30g butter
1 tbsp caster sugar
Juice of 2 limes
1 tbsp coriander, chopped

Lime and Coriander Salmon

6 x 200g salmon supremes, skin on,
  scales and bones removed
1 tbsp olive oil
Salt & pepper

Chilli Jam

Place all the ingredients in a small saucepan. Bring to the boil and simmer for 12-15 minutes. Remove from the heat and blend with a hand blender until smooth. Set to one side until needed.

Lime and Coriander Marinade

Place the butter, sugar, lime juice and coriander in a saucepan. Heat until the butter is melted and the sugar has dissolved. Remove from heat and place to one side.

Lime and Coriander Salmon

Pre-heat the oven to 170°C. Using a sharp knife, score the skin of the salmon taking care not to cut too deep. Place a large non-stick, ovenproof frying pan on the stove and heat the olive oil. Season the salmon with salt & pepper on both sides.

Place the salmon, skin side down, in the hot pan and cook for 3-4 minutes until crisp and golden brown. Gently turn the salmon over, baste the marinade over the salmon and cook in the oven for 8-10 minutes. When cooked, remove from the oven and keep warm.

Noodles

250g Udon noodles or egg noodles
Salt & pepper
1 tsp sesame oil
1 tbsp picked coriander

Stir-fried Vegetables

1 tbsp vegetable oil
1 red chilli, de-seeded and ringed
1 clove of garlic, chopped
1 tsp fresh ginger, chopped
2 medium carrots, thinly sliced
1 bunch asparagus, cut in
 half lengthways
1 red pepper, de-seeded and sliced
80g baby corn, cut in half lengthways
100g sugar snap peas, picked
1 bunch spring onions, peeled
 and chopped
1 small tin lotus root, sliced
75g white or brown beech mushrooms
 (or shiitake mushrooms)
Salt & pepper

Noodles

Bring a medium saucepan of salted water to the boil, plunge the noodles into the water and cook for 2-3 minutes. Drain through a colander. Season with salt & pepper and drizzle with sesame oil. Sprinkle with the coriander and keep them warm.

Stir-fried Vegetables

Heat a wok until very hot, add the vegetable oil, chilli, garlic and ginger and stir-fry for 30 seconds. Add the carrots, asparagus, red pepper, baby corn, sugar snap peas and stir-fry for 2 minutes. Add the spring onions, lotus root and the beech mushrooms and stir-fry for a further 2 minutes. Season the vegetables, remove from the pan and set to one side.

And finally…

Place a pile of noodles in centre of each of six large warm serving plates or bowls. Place a pile of the stir-fried vegetables on top of the noodles, place the salmon on top, then spoon the chilli jam around the plate and serve.

Mackerel Fillets on Red Chard with Sugar Snap Peas, Roasted Cherry Tomatoes and a Vermouth Velouté

Mackerel is coming back into fashion after years out in the cold, so for an on-trend dinner party try this...

Red Pepper Relish

3 red peppers
1 tsp tarragon, chopped
1 tsp black sesame seeds
½ tsp balsamic vinegar

Red Pepper Relish

Pre-heat the oven to 200°C. Place the peppers in a small roasting tin and roast in the oven for 30 minutes until they are wilted and blistered. Remove from the oven and allow to cool. Once cool, cut the peppers in half and remove the seeds, peel the skin and finely dice the flesh. Place the diced peppers in a bowl, then add the chopped tarragon, black sesame seeds and balsamic vinegar. Mix together, season and set to one side.

Fondant Potato

6 medium baking potatoes, peeled
1 tbsp vegetable oil
28g salted butter
1 litre vegetable stock (see page 207)
Pinch of saffron
Salt & pepper

Fondant Potato

Pre-heat the oven to 150°C. Using a 5cm stainless steel round cutter, cut each potato into a cylinder shape and remove the excess potato from each end. Heat the oil in a non-stick frying pan on the hob and brown one end of each of the potatoes. Place them, browned side up, in a deep roasting tin.

Bring the vegetable stock to the boil and pour over the potatoes, leaving a 1cm gap from the top of the potato. Add the butter, saffron and seasoning. Place in the oven for 1 hour until soft. Remove the potatoes from the oven, but leave them in the stock to keep warm.

Vermouth Velouté

½ tbsp olive oil
1 shallot, finely chopped
1 clove of garlic, chopped
2 tbsp vermouth (Noilly Pratt)
100ml double cream
½ litre fish velouté (see page 209)
½ lemon
Salt & pepper

Vermouth Velouté

Heat a small saucepan and add the olive oil. Cook the shallots and garlic for two minutes, without allowing them to brown. Add the vermouth, bring to the boil and reduce by half. Add the fish velouté and cream. Bring to the boil and simmer for 10 minutes. Remove from the heat and pass the sauce through a fine strainer into a clean saucepan. Add a squeeze of lemon, season with salt & pepper to taste and keep hot.

Mackerel Fillets

12 large fresh mackerel fillets, skin on,
  bones removed
50g melted butter
Salt & pepper
½ lemon

Vegetable Garnish

18 cherry tomatoes
½ tbsp olive oil
1 tbsp balsamic vinegar
100g sugar snap peas
100g baby asparagus, cut in half
25g butter
50g red chard, washed
Salt & pepper

Mackerel Fillets

Pre-heat the grill on a high setting. Using a sharp knife, score the skin of the mackerel, taking care not to cut too deep. Place the fillets, skin side up, on to a buttered tray, season and brush with the melted butter. Place under a hot grill and cook for 4-5 minutes until the skin is crisp and golden brown. Remove from the heat, squeeze the lemon over the mackerel and keep it warm.

Vegetable Garnish

Pre-heat a medium frying pan until it's hot. Add the cherry tomatoes and olive oil and cook for one minute, rolling the tomatoes around the pan to ensure they become evenly coloured. Add the balsamic vinegar and cook for 30 seconds. Remove the tomatoes from the heat and keep them warm.

Bring a small saucepan of salted water to the boil. Add the sugar snap peas and cook for 1 minute, then add the asparagus and cook for a further minute. Drain and keep them warm. Heat a medium non-stick frying pan and add the butter. Add the cooked sugar snap peas, baby asparagus and red chard and cook over a high heat for 1 minute. Season with salt & pepper, drain and keep everything warm.

And finally…

Place a pile of the sugar snap peas, asparagus and red chard at the centre of each of six large serving plates. Place three cherry tomatoes and one fondant potato around the vegetables. Place two mackerel fillets on top of the vegetables and a teaspoon of the red pepper relish on top of the mackerel, then spoon the sauce around the fish and serve.

Grilled Haddock with Pecorino and Broad Bean Potato Cakes and Roasted Red Pepper Sauce

Haddock and potato cakes make great partners. The sautéed vegetable garnish adds a little colour and texture…

Pecorino and Broad Bean Potato Cakes

1.25kg Desirée potatoes (or red potatoes)

150g broad beans, peeled

50g Pecorino, grated

Salt & pepper

Olive oil

Pecorino and Broad Bean Potato Cakes

Peel, wash and evenly chop the potatoes. Put them in a saucepan and cover with cold salted water. Bring to the boil. Simmer for 20 minutes until tender. Drain and place the potatoes into a mixing bowl. Bring a small pan of water to the boil, add the broad beans and cook for 1 minute. Remove from the water, then allow to cool down and peel.

With a fork, mix the broad beans, potatoes and Pecorino and season. Divide the mixture into six balls of equal size; gently mould and flatten until they're roughly 10cm in diameter and 2cm thick. Pan-fry in a little olive oil for 2 minutes. Using a palette knife, turn them over and fry for a further 2 minutes until golden brown and keep them warm.

Roasted Red Pepper Sauce

4 red peppers

1 shallot, peeled and chopped

1 clove of garlic, peeled and chopped

2 tbsp white wine

1 tbsp tomato purée

1 sprig tarragon

300ml vegetable stock (see page 207)

½ tbsp olive oil

Salt & pepper

Roasted Red Pepper Sauce

Pre-heat the oven to 180°C. Put the whole peppers in a roasting tin and roast for 20 minutes until soft. Remove from the oven and allow to cool.

When cool, cut in half, discard the seeds, roughly chop the peppers and put to one side. Heat a small saucepan, add the olive oil and gently fry the shallot and garlic for 1 minute until soft.

Add the white wine and reduce by half; this should take about 1 minute. Add the tomato purée, peppers, tarragon and stock. Bring to the boil and simmer for 20 minutes. Using a hand blender, whizz the sauce until smooth, then pass through a fine sieve into a clean saucepan, season and keep it warm.

Grilled Haddock

6 x 200g haddock fillets, skin on and
  bones removed
50g salted butter, melted
Sea salt
Cracked black pepper

Vegetable Garnish

9 cherry tomatoes
1 fennel bulb
1 red pepper
1 yellow pepper
1 tbsp olive oil
1 medium courgette
30 baby asparagus spears
Salt & pepper

Grilled Haddock

Pre-heat the grill. Using a sharp knife, score the skin of the haddock, taking care not to cut too deep. Place the fillets, skin side up, on a buttered tray and brush liberally with melted butter. Season with sea salt and cracked black pepper and grill for 6 minutes until the skin is crisp and golden brown and the fish is cooked all the way through. Remove from the grill and keep it warm.

Vegetable Garnish

Bring a small pan of salted water to the boil. Cut the fennel into 18 equal squares, add to the water and boil for 5 minutes. Drain and keep warm. De-seed the peppers and cut into 18 equal pieces. Wash the courgette and cut into 18 equal pieces.

Heat a large non-stick frying pan and drizzle with olive oil. Add the peppers and fennel and fry for 1 minute. Add the courgette and asparagus and fry for a further minute. Remove from the pan and keep the vegetables warm.

Cut the cherry tomatoes in half, add to the pan and cook for 1 minute. Remove from the heat and keep warm.

And finally…

Place the potato cakes in the middle of six large warm serving plates. Place the asparagus on top of the potato cake, then the haddock (skin side up). Set the rest of the vegetable garnish around the potato cake, allowing for three pieces of each pepper, courgette, fennel and cherry tomato. Spoon the sauce around the plate and serve.

Roast Fillet of Cod with Clams and a Chive, Tomato and White Wine Sauce

Fish and potatoes are a marriage made in heaven and this recipe sees them partnered with a flavoursome sauce...

Fondant Potato

6 medium baking potatoes, peeled

1 tbsp vegetable oil

28g salted butter

1 litre vegetable stock (see page 207)

Pinch of saffron

Salt & pepper

Fondant Potato

Pre-heat the oven to 150°C. Using a 5cm stainless steel round cutter, cut each potato into a cylinder shape and remove the excess potato from each end. Heat the oil in a non-stick frying pan on the hob and brown one end of each of the potatoes. Place them – browned side up – in a deep roasting tin.

Bring the vegetable stock to the boil and pour over the potatoes, leaving a 1cm gap from the top of the potato. Add the butter, saffron and seasoning. Place in the oven for 1 hour until soft. Remove the potatoes from the oven, but leave them in the stock to keep warm.

Roast Fillet of Cod

6 x 250g cod fillets, skin removed

Salt

1 tbsp olive oil

28g salted butter

1 tbsp plain flour

Roast Fillet of Cod

Pre-heat the oven to 160°C. Generously season the cod with salt – this will firm it up prior to cooking – and allow it to rest in the fridge for 10 minutes. Heat a large non-stick ovenproof frying pan on the hob. Add the olive oil and butter. Lightly dust the cod with the flour and gently lower, presentation side down, into the pan. Cook for 2 minutes on a high heat, until golden brown, then place the pan in the pre-heated oven for 12-15 minutes. When cooked, remove the pan from the oven and keep the cod warm.

Chive, Tomato and White Wine Sauce

30 parlour clams

50ml white wine

½ litre fish velouté (see page 209)

90ml double cream

1 plum tomato, de-seeded
  and diced into ½ cm pieces

1 tbsp chopped chives

½ lemon

Salt & pepper

Vegetable Garnish

12 baby carrots, peeled

40g butter

350g baby spinach

100g baby asparagus

Pinch of nutmeg, freshly grated

Salt & pepper

Chive, Tomato and White Wine Sauce

Heat a large saucepan with a tightly fitting lid. Wash the clams in plenty of salted water, removing any damaged or open clams. Drain well. Add the clams and white wine to the saucepan and replace the lid. Cook the clams until they are all open, checking all the time. Place a colander on top of a large bowl, pour the clams into the colander and catch the cooking liquor in the bowl. Remove any unopened clams and discard them. Keep the remaining clams warm.

Place the cooking liquor back in the saucepan. Add the fish velouté and the cream, then bring to the boil. Remove from the heat and pass the sauce through a fine strainer into a clean saucepan. Add the diced tomatoes, chopped chives, a squeeze of lemon juice and season with salt & pepper. Keep it warm.

Vegetable Garnish

Bring a small pan of lightly salted water to the boil and add the carrots. Cook for 2 minutes, drain and keep them warm. Heat a large frying pan. Add the butter, asparagus, spinach and carrots and cook until the spinach is wilted. Drain off any excess liquid and season with freshly grated nutmeg, salt & pepper.

And finally…

Place the vegetable garnish at the centre of six large, round, warm serving plates. Remove the fondant potato from the cooking liquor and place to one end of the plate. Carefully remove the cod from the pan and place on to the spinach, roasted side up. Spoon the sauce and place the clams in the shells (allowing five clams each) around the cod and serve.

Smoked Haddock with Welsh Rarebit Crust, Asparagus Ravioli and Pesto Cream Sauce

Britain meets Italy in this delicious dish which sees subtle flavours of the haddock, complemented by the fragrant pesto sauce…

Fresh Pasta

300g pasta flour (from any high street
   supermarket)
3 large eggs
8 egg yolks

Asparagus Ravioli

(makes approximately 1 litre)
12 asparagus spears
1 tbsp olive oil
2 shallots, finely chopped
1 clove of garlic, chopped
150ml double cream
1 tbsp Pecorino, grated
Salt & pepper
350g fresh pasta
1 beaten egg

Fresh Pasta

Place the flour on a clean surface. Make a well in the centre and add the large eggs and the egg yolks. With a fork, break up the eggs as you bring in the flour. Stir with the fork until you have a dough that you can work with your hands. Knead well until you have a smooth and elastic dough. Wrap the dough in clingfilm and leave in the fridge for at least half an hour.

Asparagus Ravioli

Cut the asparagus into small pieces and discard the woody end. Heat the olive oil in a medium saucepan and cook the shallots and garlic for 2 minutes without allowing them to brown. Add the asparagus and cook for a further 1 minute. Add the cream and simmer for 5 minutes until it has reduced and the asparagus has cooked through. Add the Pecorino, season and cool.

Divide the pasta in half and keep the half you are not using covered. Working with one piece at a time, flatten it out with your hands, dust it with flour and put it through the thickest setting on a pasta machine (you can buy these from any cookware shop). Then fold it in half and put it through the machine again. Repeat this process several times as it makes the pasta easier to work with. Continue lightly dusting the pasta with flour and move the settings lower each time, so the pasta will become thinner. You should put it through each setting twice, resting it between each rolling for about a minute. Do this until you have reached the desired thickness, which is around 2mm. Lay one prepared pasta sheet on to a floured surface and brush all over with beaten egg. Place a dessertspoon of asparagus filling 6cm apart along the length of the pasta sheet. Place the other sheet of pasta over the asparagus filling and lightly press to remove any air pockets. Cut the raviolis out with a 6cm round pastry cutter. Pinch the edge of each ravioli to make sure they are sealed. Repeat the process until you have 18 raviolis. Refrigerate until needed.

Welsh Rarebit

30g butter

30g plain flour

1 tsp English mustard powder

250ml milk

200g mature Cheddar, grated

28g white breadcrumbs

2 medium egg yolks

1 tsp Worcestershire sauce

Salt & pepper

Welsh Rarebit

Melt the butter in a small, heavy-bottomed saucepan. Add the flour and mix with a wooden spoon. Cook on a gentle heat for 1 minute. Add the mustard powder and mix thoroughly, then gradually add the cold milk and mix until smooth. Bring to the boil and allow it to simmer for a few minutes. Add the grated cheese and allow it to melt slowly over a gentle heat, stirring continuously, until you have a smooth mixture. Stir in the fresh white breadcrumbs and the egg yolks and immediately remove from the heat. Add the Worcestershire sauce. Season with salt & pepper and allow to cool. Refrigerate until needed.

Pesto Cream Sauce

½ tbsp olive oil

1 shallot, chopped

1 clove of garlic, chopped

2 tbsp white wine

½ litre fish velouté (see page 209)

100ml double cream

1 tbsp green pesto

½ lemon, squeezed

Salt & pepper

Pesto Cream Sauce

Heat the olive oil in a small saucepan. Add the shallots and garlic and cook over a medium heat for 2 minutes, not allowing them to brown. Add the white wine and bring to the boil. Add the fish velouté and double cream and bring back to the boil. Simmer for 10 minutes. Remove from the heat and pass through a fine strainer into a clean saucepan. Add the green pesto and lemon juice. Season to taste and keep it warm.

Smoked Haddock

6 x 200g smoked haddock fillets

250g Welsh rarebit (prepared earlier)

Smoked Haddock

Pre-heat the oven to 180°C and pre-heat the grill to a high setting. Place the haddock in a roasting tray.

Separate the rarebit into six equal pieces, then pat out in your hands until it is 2-3mm thick and lay it on top of the haddock, making sure the fillets are completely covered. Place in a hot oven for 7-8 minutes until cooked. Remove from the oven and place under the hot grill to colour and glaze the rarebit. Remove from the grill and keep it warm.

Vegetable Garnish

2 plum tomatoes
1 medium leek
1 fennel bulb
12 large asparagus spears
100g mange tout
1 tbsp olive oil
40g butter
Salt & pepper

Vegetable Garnish

Quarter the plum tomatoes lengthways and remove the seeds and then cut each quarter into three. Cut the leek and fennel bulb into fine 2.5cm strips. Remove the woody end of the asparagus and cut in half lengthways. Bring a small pan of salted water to the boil, then add the asparagus and cook for 1 minute. Drain and keep warm.

Heat the olive oil and butter in a medium non-stick frying-pan, add the fennel, leek, asparagus and mange tout and cook over a high heat for 2 minutes. Add the tomatoes, season, remove from the heat and keep them warm.

And finally…

Bring a large pan of salted water to the boil. Add the ravioli, a tablespoon of olive oil and cook for 3-4 minutes. Remove the ravioli from the water and drain well.

Place three ravioli at the centre of six large warm serving plates or bowls. Place a pile of vegetables on top of the ravioli and spoon over the pesto cream sauce. Place the haddock on top of the vegetables and serve.

Baked Halibut with a Herb and Gruyère Crust, Carrot Mash, Braised Leeks and Lemon Sauce

A comforting dish, perfect as a starter or a main course. Simply adjust the amounts accordingly…

Carrot Mash

2 large baking potatoes
750g whole carrots
80g butter
Sea salt
Freshly ground black pepper

Carrot Mash

Peel the potatoes and carrots and cut them into equal sizes. Bring a large pan of salted water to the boil and cook the carrots and potatoes for 15 minutes until they're soft.

Remove from the heat and drain through a colander. Place the potatoes and carrots back in the saucepan and – using a potato masher – mash them until they are smooth. Place the pan back on the stove and heat the mash for 5 minutes, stirring continuously to allow most of the liquid to evaporate. Stir in the butter. Remove the pan from the heat. Season the mash with the sea salt and ground black pepper and keep it warm.

Lemon Sauce

½ tbsp olive oil
1 shallot, peeled and chopped
1 clove of garlic, chopped
2 tbsp white wine
½ litre fish velouté (see page 209)
100ml cream
1 lemon
Salt & pepper
1 tbsp chives, finely cut

Lemon Sauce

Heat the olive oil in a medium saucepan and gently cook the shallot and garlic for 2 minutes, ensuring they don't brown. Add the wine and reduce by half. Pour in the fish velouté, bring to the boil and simmer for 5 minutes.

Add the cream and a squeeze of lemon. Season with salt & pepper and heat for a further minute. Remove the saucepan from the heat. Pass the sauce through a fine sieve into a clean container, add the chives and keep it warm.

Halibut with Herb and Gruyère Crust

1 small ciabatta loaf, diced
75g gruyère, grated
Zest of 1 lemon
1 tbsp parsley, chopped
1 tbsp chives, chopped
Salt & pepper
6 x 200g fresh halibut, evenly cut to
  2.5cm fillets, skin removed
50g melted butter

Vegetable Garnish

2 red peppers
1 tbsp olive oil
1 large leek, cut into rings and washed
100ml vegetable stock
Salt & pepper

Halibut with Herb and Gruyère Crust

Pre-heat the oven to 180°C. Roughly cut up the ciabatta. Place the diced bread in a blender and blitz until you have large breadcrumbs, then empty into a mixing bowl.

Add the gruyère, lemon zest, parsley and chives into the bowl and gently combine all the ingredients. Season with salt & pepper and set to one side. Place the halibut on to a large buttered baking tray and brush with some of the melted butter. Season with salt & pepper. Divide the breadcrumb mix into six and sprinkle it liberally over each of the halibut fillets and drizzle with butter.

When all the fillets are covered in the crumb mix, place the tray in the oven and cook for 12-15 minutes until the breadcrumb mix is brown and the fish is cooked all the way through. Remove the halibut from the oven and keep it warm.

Vegetable Garnish

Cut the red peppers in half, de-seed them and chop them into large strips. Heat the olive oil in a large, non-stick frying pan. Add the peppers and cook over a medium heat for 2 minutes. Add the leeks and the vegetable stock and turn up the heat. Reduce the vegetable stock until it has evaporated and the leeks are cooked. Season with salt & pepper and keep it warm.

And finally…

Place a large spoonful of the carrot mash on to six large, warm serving bowls or plates. Place a spoonful of the vegetable garnish to one side of the carrot mash and lay a piece of halibut on top of both the carrot mash and vegetables. Spoon the sauce around the halibut and serve.

Seared Turbot with an Asparagus Trio and Herb Risotto

Fish and asparagus are a wonderful combination. Light and delicious, just perfect for a summer dish…

Tomato and Herb Relish

½ bunch tarragon, chopped
½ bunch basil
100ml olive oil
1 plum tomato
1 small red onion, finely chopped
Salt & pepper

Smoked Asparagus Velouté

Olive oil
1 shallot, finely chopped
1 clove of garlic, chopped
4 asparagus spears, chopped
2 slices smoked salmon
2 tbsp white wine
½ litre fish velouté (see page 209)
100ml double cream
Salt & pepper

Tomato and Herb Relish

Put the herbs and the olive oil in a bowl and blend with a hand blender until smooth. Cut the tomato in four, remove the seeds and finely dice. Add the tomato and onion to the herb oil, season with salt & pepper and leave to infuse until needed.

Smoked Asparagus Velouté

Warm a small saucepan on the hob. Add the olive oil, shallot and garlic and cook on a medium heat for 1 minute without colour. Add the asparagus and smoked salmon and cook for a further 3 minutes. Add the white wine, the fish velouté and cream, and simmer for 5 minutes. Remove from the heat, take the salmon out and discard. Blend the sauce with a hand blender until smooth. Pass through a fine strainer into a clean saucepan and keep warm. Season to taste.

Herb Risotto

1 tbsp olive oil

50g butter

2 shallots, peeled and finely chopped

2 cloves of garlic, finely chopped

400g risotto rice (eg Arborio)

2 tbsp white wine

1 litre vegetable stock, hot (see page 207)

1 tbsp fresh Parmesan, grated

1 tbsp chopped parsley

Salt & pepper

Vegetable Garnish

2 beetroots

50g of butter

12 white asparagus spears

100g baby asparagus

12 purple asparagus spears

Salt & pepper

Herb Risotto

Heat a medium saucepan on the hob. Add the olive oil, 25g of the butter, shallots and garlic and cook over a medium heat for 1 minute, without colour. Add the rice and stir so it is completely coated. Cook for a minute or so until the rice becomes opaque. Add the wine and cook for another minute until the wine is completely absorbed.

Turn down the heat and begin gradually adding the stock, a ladle at a time. Stir until the stock is absorbed, before adding more. It should take around 15 minutes for all the stock to be used and for the rice to be cooked al dente.

To finish, stir in the remaining butter, Parmesan, chopped parsley and season with salt & pepper. Keep the risotto warm.

Vegetable Garnish

Peel the beetroot and using a small Solfrino cutter (small melon-baller) cut out around 30 small balls. Warm 25g of butter in a small frying pan and sauté the beetroot until hot, season and keep it warm. Bring a small pot of salted water to the boil. Add the white asparagus and cook for 2 minutes, then add the baby and purple asparagus and cook for a further minute, before draining in a colander. Keep it warm.

Heat a medium frying pan, add the remaining butter and gently sauté the three types of asparagus for one minute. Season, drain and keep them warm.

Seared Turbot

6 x 175g turbot fillets, skin removed

1 tbsp olive oil

55g of butter

½ lemon

Salt & pepper

Seared Turbot

Heat the olive oil in a large non-stick frying pan and cook the fish over a medium heat for 3 minutes on each side. Towards the end of cooking, add the butter and baste the fish for one minute. Squeeze the lemon over the fish and season with salt & pepper. Remove from the heat and keep it warm.

And finally…

Place a large spoon of the risotto at the centre of six large plates or pasta bowls. Place the baby asparagus over the risotto followed by two spears of the white and purple asparagus and the pan-fried turbot. Spoon the sauce around the risotto, garnish with the beetroot balls and finish with a spoon of the tomato and herb relish on top of the turbot.

Sea Bream on Asian Greens with Crab Wontons and Pea Shoot Coconut Sauce

This has a delicious, clean eastern feel and, although a little fiddly, looks very impressive. Make a simple starter and pudding and concentrate on this dish to really blow your guests away…

Crab Wontons

1 tbsp olive oil
1 red chilli, de-seeded and chopped
1 tsp ground coriander
2 cloves of garlic, peeled and chopped
200g white crabmeat
1 sprig coriander, finely chopped
1 sprig basil, finely chopped
30ml lobster sauce (see page 32)
12 wonton wrappers
1 egg
Salt & pepper

Crab Wontons

Heat the olive oil in a medium non-stick frying pan. Add the red chilli, ground coriander and the garlic and cook on a medium heat for 2 minutes. Remove from the pan, place on a clean plate and refrigerate until cold.

In a separate bowl, gently mix together the crabmeat, chopped coriander, basil, lobster sauce and the chilled red chilli and garlic. Season and set to one side.

Place six of the wonton wrappers on to a lightly floured work surface and place 2 tsp of the crab mixture at the centre of each. Brush the egg around the edge and place another wonton wrapper on top. In the palm of your hands, gently squeeze around the edges to seal and make sure no excess air remains.

At this point cut the wrapper with a round pastry cutter or leave them as a square shape. Place on a clean tray and refrigerate until needed.

Asian Greens

1 red pepper, de-seeded

1 yellow pepper, de-seeded

1 green pepper, de-seeded

12 baby leeks

2 carrots, peeled

100g baby corn

3 medium bok choi

2 tbsp olive oil

1 tbsp butter

Salt & pepper

Asian Greens

Cut each of the peppers into 12 equal pieces and set to one side. Peel down one layer of the leek and wash off any remaining dirt. Slice the carrots in half lengthways and then slice at an angle to achieve long, thin, half-moon shapes. Leave to one side. Slice the baby corn in half lengthways and place with the other vegetables. Slice the bok choi in half lengthways, then wash off the dirt and leave to drain on kitchen roll.

Heat a large, non-stick frying pan on the stove. Add 1 tbsp of olive oil. When it's hot add the peppers. Cook on a high heat for 3 minutes until lightly golden. Remove from the heat and keep warm. Return the pan to the stove, heat 1 tbsp of olive oil and add the carrots, and cook for 2 minutes. Add the baby corn and cook them both for a further 3 minutes. Remove from the pan and keep warm. Bring a small pan of salted water to the boil, put in the bok choi and simmer for 1 minute. Take the pan off the heat, drain through a colander, season, and keep warm.

Pea Shoot Coconut Sauce

1 tbsp olive oil

2 cloves of garlic, chopped

1 red chilli, chopped

1 lemongrass stalk, chopped

500ml coconut milk

150g petits pois (frozen is fine)

50g pea shoots

Salt & pepper

Pea Shoot Coconut Sauce

Heat the olive oil in a medium saucepan. Add the garlic, chilli and lemongrass and cook for 2 minutes until soft. Pour in the coconut milk and bring to the boil. Reduce by a quarter; this should take around 10 minutes. Add the petits pois and pea shoots and simmer for 2 minutes. Remove from the heat and, using a hand blender, blitz until smooth. Pass through a fine sieve into a suitable container, season according to taste and keep warm.

Sea Bream

1 tbsp olive oil

25g salted butter

Salt & pepper

6 x 200g medium sea bream fillets, skin on
   and pin-boned

Sea Bream

Heat the olive oil and butter in a large non-stick frying pan. Season and gently fry the sea bream fillets, skin side down, for 3 minutes until they are golden brown. Carefully turn over the fillets and continue the process on the other side. Remove from the heat and keep warm.

And finally…

Place a medium pot of salted water on the stove and bring to the boil. Add the wontons and simmer for 3 minutes. Remove from the water drain on some kitchen roll.

Take six large warm serving plates and place two of the wontons at the side of each. Arrange the peppers, leeks, corn and carrots in a neat pile in the centre of the plate. Lay one piece of bok choi on top of the vegetables and place the seared sea bream on top of the bok choi. Spoon around the sauce, making sure to cover the wontons, and serve.

Pan-fried Fillet of Sea Bass on Herb Linguine with Shellfish Minestrone

A dish that captures the flavours of the Mediterranean...

Aioli

50g Desirée Potatoes

2 cloves of garlic, peeled and crushed

2 medium eggs

25ml olive oil

Salt & pepper

Aioli

Peel the potatoes and cut them into large cubes. Put them in a saucepan and cover with cold water and bring to the boil. Cook the potatoes until they're tender. Drain and allow them to cool. Hard-boil the eggs and then cool them off under cold running water. Peel the eggs and remove the yolk. Place the potato, garlic and hard-boiled yolk into a food processor and blend until smooth, gradually adding the olive oil. The aioli should be a smooth mayonnaise consistency. Season with salt & pepper and refrigerate until you need it.

Focaccia Croute

1 medium focaccia loaf

1 tbsp extra-virgin olive oil

1 tbsp dried mixed herbs

1 tsp sesame seeds

1 tsp Maldon salt

Focaccia Croute

Pre-heat the oven to 160°C. Cut the focaccia into six thin slices and lay them on greaseproof paper on a baking sheet. Drizzle with olive oil and sprinkle with the mixed herbs and sesame seeds and salt. Bake in the oven for 12 minutes until golden brown. Allow to cool.

Sun-dried Tomato Sauce

6 plum tomatoes, cut in half

Olive oil

3 large shallots, finely chopped

2 sticks celery, finely chopped

2 cloves of garlic, peeled and chopped

2 tbsp white wine

1 tbsp tomato purée

80g sun-blushed or sun-dried tomatoes

600ml fish stock (see page 208)

2 sprigs tarragon

1 tsp balsamic vinegar

Salt & pepper

Sun-dried Tomato Sauce

Pre-heat the oven to 180°C. Place the plum tomatoes in a small ovenproof dish, drizzle with olive oil, season and roast in the oven for 30 minutes. Heat a small saucepan. Add some olive oil, the shallots, celery and garlic and cook over a medium heat for 1 minute, without allowing them to brown. Add the wine and reduce by half. Add the tomato purée, the sun-blushed and the oven-roasted tomatoes and cook for a further 2 minutes.

Add the fish stock and tarragon, bring to the boil and simmer for 10 minutes. Remove from the heat and blend with a hand blender until it's smooth. Pass the sauce through a fine strainer into a clean saucepan. Add the balsamic vinegar season with salt & pepper and keep warm. If the sauce is too thick, thin it down with a little water.

Squid

200g squid, cleaned

Herb Linguine

1 red pepper, de-seeded
1 yellow pepper, de-seeded
½ leek
1 courgette
450g dried linguine
3 tbsp olive oil
1 tsp dill, chopped
1 tsp parsley, chopped
1 tsp chives, chopped
Salt & pepper
150g fresh cooked shelled prawns
175g fresh mussels

Squid

A good fishmonger will prepare the squid for you. If you have to do it yourself, hold the body in one hand and feel around inside the body for the cartilage (which feels a little like hard plastic). Gently pull it out, remove any black skin and thoroughly wash the remaining tube until it is completely white. Dry well and slice into thin rings. Refridgerate until ready to use.

Herb Linguine

Cut the peppers into 1cm square dice and set to one side. Wash and dry the leek and cut it into 1cm square dice. Cut the courgette in half, then into quarters lengthways, and then into 1cm dice and leave to one side. Bring a large pan of salted water to the boil and add the linguine. Cook as per the instructions on the packet. Drain well and drizzle with 1 tbsp olive oil, sprinkle with the herbs, season with salt & pepper and keep it warm.

Heat a large non-stick frying pan on the stove, add 1 tbsp olive oil and cook the vegetables for two minutes, then add the leeks and cook for a further 1 minute. Remove from the pan and keep them warm. Wash the mussels in plenty of salted water, removing any that are damaged or opened. Drain well and remove the beards from the edge of the shells. Heat a large saucepan with a tight fitting lid, add the white wine and mussels to the saucepan and cover with the lid.

Cook the mussels until they are open. Place a colander on top of a large bowl and pour the mussels into it. Remove any unopened mussels and discard them. Put aside six mussels in their shells for the garnish. Remove the remaining mussels from their shells and keep them warm. Heat a large non-stick frying pan on the hob until it's hot and add the remaining olive oil. Add the squid and cook for 30 seconds, then add the prawns and mussels and cook for a further minute. Add the cooked vegetables and the linguine, season and keep them warm.

Sea Bass

1 tbsp olive oil

1 tbsp salted butter

6 x 200g sea bass fillets, skin on and
  pin-boned

Sea Bass

Heat a large non-stick frying pan, add the olive oil and then
the butter. Place the sea bass fillets skin side down and gently
fry for 3 minutes until they are golden brown. Carefully turn
over the fillets and continue the process on the other side.
Remove from the heat and keep them warm.

And finally…

Divide the linguine between six large, warm, serving bowls. As
the picture shows, place the seafood and vegetable garnish
over and around the linguine. Spoon the sauce over and
around the linguine and place the sea bass on top. Place a
teaspoon of the aioli on top of the sea bass, then lean the
foccacia croute up the side and set one mussel in the shell
as pictured.

Roast Cod and Braised Root Vegetables with a Mussel and Chardonnay Sauce

This dish is light and fragrant and works well with halibut or turbot in place of cod...

Braised Root Vegetables

1 tsp turmeric

450g new potatoes, washed

2 medium carrots, peeled

½ swede, peeled

1 medium sweet potato, peeled

½ litre vegetable stock (see page 207)

1 sprig thyme

100g frozen peas

1 small leek, washed and diced

50g butter

1 tbsp olive oil

Salt & pepper

Braised Root Vegetables

Bring a small pot of salted water to the boil and add the turmeric. Cut the new potatoes in half lengthways and boil for 15 minutes until tender. Remove from the water and allow to cool. Pre-heat a medium frying pan. Dice the carrot, swede and sweet potato into even 1cm dice. Add a knob of butter to the pan, add the vegetables and fry over a medium heat for 2 minutes until they're lightly coloured. Add the vegetable stock and thyme to the carrots, swede and sweet potato and cook for 5 minutes. Then add the peas and the diced leek and simmer gently for 2 minutes, then strain off any excess liquid. Season and keep them warm.

Heat a non-stick frying pan, add the butter, olive oil and the cooked new potatoes and gently fry for 2 minutes on each side until golden brown. Remove the potatoes from the pan and drain on kitchen roll. Season and them keep warm.

Chardonnay Sauce

15g butter

1 shallot, peeled and chopped

1 clove of garlic, chopped

75ml Chardonnay

½ litre fish velouté

100ml double cream

400g fresh mussels

½ lemon

Salt & pepper

Chardonnay Sauce

Heat a small saucepan and add the butter. Add the shallots and garlic and cook over a medium heat for 2 minutes, not allowing them to colour. Add the white wine, reduce by half, then add the fish velouté and double cream. Simmer for 10 minutes.

Wash the mussels in plenty of salted water removing any damaged or opened mussels. Drain well and pull out the beards from the edges of the shells. Heat a large saucepan with a tight fitting lid, add the white wine and mussels to the saucepan and replace the lid. Cook the mussels until they are all open. Place a colander on top of a large bowl, pour the mussels into the colander and remove any unopened mussels and discard them. Remove the mussels from the shells and keep warm. Pass the sauce through a fine strainer into a clean saucepan. Bring to the boil and add the mussels. Add a squeeze of lemon and the salt & pepper and remove from the stove and keep warm.

Roast Cod

6 x 250g grade-A cod fillets, skin on
Salt & pepper
1 tbsp olive oil
1 tbsp plain flour
40g butter
½ lemon

Roast Cod

Pre-heat the oven to 160°C. Season the cod fillets with salt & pepper, place on a tray and refrigerate for 10 minutes to firm the flesh. Heat a large, non-stick, ovenproof frying pan and add the olive oil. Lightly dust the skin of the cod fillets with flour and gently lower into the pan, skin side down. Cook over a high heat for 3-4 minutes until the skin is golden brown.

Turn the cod fillets, add the butter and baste the cod. Leaving the cod in the frying pan, place in the oven for 12-15 minutes until cooked. Remove from the oven, squeeze over the lemon juice and keep the fish warm.

Spinach and Red Chard

40g butter
250g baby spinach, washed
50g red chard, washed
Salt & pepper
Fresh nutmeg

Spinach and Red Chard

Heat a large non-stick frying pan and add the butter. Add the spinach and red chard and cook over a high heat for 2 minutes until the leaves are wilted. Season with salt & pepper and grate over a little nutmeg. Drain and remove from the heat.

And finally…

Place a pile of spinach and red chard at the centre of six large plates or pasta bowls. Place the roasted cod on top. Spoon the root vegetables over the cod. Place three pan-fried new potatoes around the cod, spoon the mussel sauce over the cod and around the vegetables and serve.

Griddled Loin of Tuna with Basmati and Wild Camargue Rice and Thai Fish Broth

The simplicity of the griddled tuna and the wonderful mix of flavours in the Thai broth complement each other superbly…

Basmati and Red Camargue Rice

60g Camargue rice

150g Basmati & wild rice

150g long-grain rice

1 tbsp turmeric

Salt

Basmati and Red Camargue Rice

Bring a small pan of salted water to the boil and add the Camargue rice. Simmer and cook for 20-25 minutes. Remove from the heat, strain through a colander and keep it warm.

In another pan of boiling salted water, cook the wild and Basmati rice for 20 minutes, drain through a colander and keep hot. Bring a small saucepan of salted water to the boil, add the turmeric and long-grain rice and cook for 14 minutes. Remove from the heat, strain through a colander and keep warm. Mix all the varieties of rice together in a clean container and keep warm until needed.

Thai Fish Broth

1 tbsp vegetable oil

10g fresh ginger, chopped

1 red chilli, de-seeded and chopped

3 cloves of garlic, chopped

1 lemongrass stalk, chopped

300ml coconut milk

200ml fish velouté (see page 209)

25g basil

1 lime

Salt & pepper

25g coriander, chopped

Thai Fish Broth

Heat a medium saucepan and add the vegetable oil. Place the ginger, red chilli, garlic and lemongrass in the pan and cook for 2 minutes without allowing them to brown. Pour in the coconut milk, fish velouté and basil, bring to the boil and then simmer for 10 minutes. Remove from the heat and, using a hand blender, blitz the broth until it's smooth. Squeeze in the lime and season to taste. Pass through a fine strainer into a clean saucepan, add the coriander and keep it warm until it's needed.

Griddled Tuna

6 x 200g tuna steaks
1 tbsp olive oil
Salt & pepper
1 lime

Vegetable Garnish

1 red pepper, de-seeded
1 yellow pepper, de-seeded
60g shiitake mushrooms
2 spring onions
1 red onion, peeled
12 baby corn
3 heads of bok choi
1 tbsp olive oil
Salt & pepper

Griddled Tuna

Heat a medium grill pan on the hob until it is hot. Drizzle the tuna steaks with the olive oil, season and place them in the grill pan. Cook for 2 minutes, then gently lift the tuna and turn it 45°, then place it back on the griddle on the same side and cook for a further 2 minutes to give the char-grilled look as pictured on page 138.

Gently turn over the tuna and cook for a further 3-4 minutes. The tuna should remain a little pink in the centre. If you prefer your tuna well done, allow it to cook for a further 2-3 minutes on both sides. Remove from the grill pan, squeeze a little lime over the tuna steaks and keep them warm.

Vegetable Garnish

Thinly slice the peppers, mushrooms, spring onions and red onion and set to one side. Cut the baby corn in half, lengthways and set to one side. Slice the bok choi lengthways in half, wash them and then drop them into boiling water and cook for 2 minutes. Drain and place on kitchen roll.

Heat a large frying pan, add the olive oil and cook the peppers, red onion and baby corn for 2 minutes. Then add the bok choi spring onions and mushrooms and cook for a further 2 minutes, season with salt & pepper. Remove the pan from the heat and keep everything warm.

And finally…

Place a large spoon of the mixed rice to one side of each of six large, warm serving bowls. Place a pile of the vegetable garnish on to the other side with one piece of bok choi on top. Place the char-grilled tuna on top of the rice, spoon the sauce around the tuna and serve.

Seared Sea Bass and Braised Oxtail Ravioli Scented with Truffle Oil

Although slightly more time consuming, the results of this recipe are well worth the effort. Much can be done in advance and there are a number of ways you can make it easier…

Fresh Pasta

300g pasta flour

3 large eggs

8 egg yolks

Braised Oxtail Ravioli

2 tbsp olive oil

125g plain flour

Salt & pepper

1 kg oxtail

150g carrots, peeled and roughly
  chopped

1 large onion, roughly chopped

2 sticks celery, roughly chopped

1 sprig thyme

2 cloves of garlic, crushed

2 tbsp tomato purée

200ml red wine

1 litre brown chicken stock
  (see page 208)

Fresh Pasta

Place the flour on a clean surface. Make a well in the centre and add all of the large eggs and the egg yolks. With a fork, break up the eggs as you bring in the flour, stir with the fork until you have a dough that you can work with your hands. Knead well until you have a smooth and elastic dough. Wrap the dough in clingfilm and leave in the fridge for at least 30 minutes.

Braised Oxtail Ravioli

Pre-heat the oven to 160°C. Heat 1 tbsp of olive oil in a large ovenproof casserole dish on the hob. Pour the flour on to a plate and season it with salt & pepper. Place the oxtail in the flour until coated on both sides. Shake any excess flour back on to the plate – keeping it aside for later – and place the oxtail in the casserole dish. Cook for 3 minutes on each side until golden brown and then remove from the casseroles dish and place on a tray.

Do not clean the casserole dish. Roughly chop the carrots, onion and celery. Place the casserole dish back on the hob and heat another tbsp of olive oil. Add the chopped vegetables, thyme and garlic. Cook for 5 minutes until the vegetables are golden brown all over, then add 55g of the seasoned flour and stir in well.

Add tomato purée and mix in well, then the red wine, chicken stock and bring to boil. Remove from the heat, add the oxtail and cover with a lid.

Place the oxtail in the pre-heated oven for approximately 3 hours and cook until the meat falls away from the bone, checking every 30 minutes to prevent it from burning.

Remove the oxtail from the liquor, set on a plate and allow to cool then refrigerate. Pass the liquor through a fine strainer into a medium saucepan, put it on a medium heat and reduce it by two thirds to give it a rich sauce; this should take around 20 minutes. Season to taste. Leave the sauce on the side to cool before refrigerating.

When the oxtail has cooled, pull the meat away from the bone, discarding any fat and gristle. Chop the meat finely and put it into a bowl, then add 70ml of the oxtail sauce to create a thick paste for the ravioli filling.

Making the Ravioli

Divide the pasta in two and keep the half you are not using covered. Working with one piece at a time, flatten it out with your hands, dust it with flour and put it through the thickest setting on a pasta machine (you can buy these from any cookware shop).

Then fold it in half and put it through the machine again. Repeat this process several times as it makes the pasta easier to work with. Continue lightly dusting the pasta with flour and move the settings lower each time, so the pasta will become thinner. You should put it through each setting twice, resting it between each rolling for about a minute. Do this until you have reached the desired thickness, which is around 2mm.

Lay the prepared pasta sheet on to a clean floured surface and cut it into six 10cm squares. Repeat with the second sheet of pasta.

Add a generous heaped teaspoon of oxtail filling to the middle of the square. Brush water around the edges of the pasta with a pastry brush. Place another square on top and in the palm of your hands, gently squeeze around the edges to seal and extract any excess air. This will ensure the ravioli won't split.

Cut each parcel with a 7.5cm round pastry cutter. Place them on a flour-dusted tray in the fridge until needed.

Cep Velouté

1 tbsp olive oil
100g shallots, peeled and chopped
80g dried ceps
100ml white wine
450ml fish velouté (see page 209)

Sea Bass

1 tbsp olive oil
1 tbsp salted butter
Salt & pepper
6 x 200g sea bass fillets, skin on

Vegetable Garnish

Juice of 1 lemon
6 whole baby fennel
150g samphire
2 tbsp olive oil
3 Portobello mushrooms, cut in half
1 tbsp butter
12 cherry tomatoes

Cep Velouté

Heat the olive oil in a medium saucepan, add the shallots and gently cook, not allowing them to brown. Add the ceps and white wine and reduce the wine by half; this should take about 3 minutes.

Add the velouté and gently bring to the boil. Reduce the heat and leave to cook for a further 10 minutes, stirring every couple of minutes. This will infuse all the flavours. Pass through a fine sieve and keep warm.

Sea Bass

Heat a large non-stick frying pan and add the olive oil and butter. Season and gently fry the sea bass, skin-side down, for 3 minutes until golden brown. Carefully turn the fillets over and cook the other side. Remove from the heat and keep warm.

Vegetable Garnish

Place a pan of salted water on the stove and bring to the boil. Add the lemon juice and the fennel and cook for 15 minutes or until soft. Remove the fennel, cut it in half and keep to one side. In the same pan, add the samphire and cook for 1 minute.

Place the sliced Portobello mushrooms, brushed with a little olive oil, under the grill for 2 minutes, cooking them on both sides. Remove and keep warm.

Heat half the olive oil and butter in a small non-stick frying pan. Add the tomatoes and cook for 1 minute before adding the fennel and samphire. Cook for a further minute until the garnish is warmed through.

And finally…

Bring a large pan of salted water to the boil, add the ravioli, simmer and cook for 3-4 minutes. Remove from the water, drizzle the truffle oil over the ravioli and keep it warm.

To assemble the dish, take six large, warm plates and place the samphire in the centre of each. Place the ravioli on the top. Place the sea bass on top of the samphire, just sitting on the side of the ravioli. Lean the fennel and Portobello mushrooms on the side of the sea bass and place the cherry tomatoes at the top of the plate. Take the velouté and pass through a fine strainer. Spoon around the sea bass with a little of the sauce drizzled over the ravioli.

We are constantly amazed at the range of quality food offered by The NEC team.

The whole team is a pleasure to work with and always striving for improvements in quality and service. A huge undertaking for any catering operation, but quite remarkable when one considers the scale and diversity of their operations.

We were particularly delighted with the way the team took on the complete running of our Great British menu restaurant at last year's BBC summer food festival, attracting favourable comment from many leading chefs.

Simon Daukes
Group Managing Director, Haymarket Exhibitions and BBC Haymarket Exhibitions

Thyme Oven-baked Butternut Squash with Wild Mushroom Risotto and a Pumpkin Seed Biscuit

This dish is sure to become a real winter dinner party favourite...

Baked Butternut Squash

3 small butternut squash

2 tbsp olive oil

1 sprig fresh thyme

Salt & pepper

Baked Butternut Squash

Pre-heat the oven to 160°C. Cut the squash in half lengthways and scoop out the seeds using a soup spoon. Lay the butternut squash flat side up and carefully make deep "criss-cross" incisions into the flesh, ensuring you don't cut all the way through.

Pre-heat a large non-stick ovenproof frying pan. Add the olive oil and place the squash flat side down in the pan. Cook for 2 minutes or until it's golden brown. Turn over the squash and sprinkle over the fresh thyme and salt & pepper.

Place the pan in the oven and bake the squash for 20-25 minutes until cooked. Remove from the oven and keep it warm.

Wild Mushroom Risotto

1 tbsp olive oil

2 shallots, peeled and finely chopped

2 cloves of garlic, finely chopped

300g risotto rice (Arborio rice)

60ml white wine

900ml vegetable stock (see page 207)

300g wild mushrooms, brushed and cleaned

40g butter, sliced

350g shaved Parmesan

1 tbsp parsley, chopped

Salt & pepper

Wild Mushroom Risotto

Heat a medium saucepan, add the olive oil, shallots and garlic and cook over a medium heat for 1 minute, without browning. Add the rice and cook for a further minute, stirring continuously, until it becomes opaque.

Add the white wine and cook for a minute, until the wine is completely absorbed. Gradually add the stock to the rice, stirring all the time, until it has all been used. This should take 12-15 minutes and the rice should have a slight bite.

Pre-heat a medium frying pan. Add the olive oil and cook the mushrooms for 3 minutes. Remove the mushrooms from the heat and drain on kitchen roll. Add the cooked mushrooms to the risotto. Stir in the butter, Parmesan and chopped parsley, and season with salt & pepper. Keep the risotto warm until you need it.

Pumpkin Seed Biscuit

75g pumpkin seeds
2 medium sheets of filo pastry
1 egg yolk

Pumpkin Seed Biscuit

Pre-heat the oven to 170°C. Line a baking tray with non-stick parchment paper. Place one sheet of filo pastry on to the paper and lightly brush with the egg yolk. Lay the other piece of pastry on and brush with the remaining egg yolk. Sprinkle the pumpkin seeds evenly over the top of the pastry and bake in the oven for 3-4 minutes or until it's golden brown. Remove from the oven and allow it to cool.

Butternut Squash Sauce

1 tbsp olive oil
1 clove of garlic, finely chopped
1 shallot, peeled and chopped
20ml white wine
350g butternut squash, peeled,
  de-seeded and roughly chopped
750ml vegetable stock (see page 207)
Salt & pepper

Butternut Squash Sauce

Place a medium saucepan on the hob. Heat the olive oil. Add the garlic and shallot and cook, over a low heat, for 2 minutes until soft, but ensure you don't let them brown.

Add the white wine and reduce by half; this should take a couple of minutes. Add the butternut squash and cook for a further 2 minutes. Pour in the vegetable stock, bring to the boil and cook for a further 20 minutes until soft.

Remove the squash from the pan – keeping aside the liquid – and blitz in a liquidiser. Pass it through a fine sieve into a clean saucepan. Season with salt & pepper and keep it warm. If the sauce appears too thick add a little of the squash liquor to thin it down.

Garnish

6 asparagus spears

1 tbsp olive oil

100g Parmesan shavings

Garnish

Pre-heat a grill-pan on the hob. Bring a medium saucepan of water to the boil and cook the asparagus for 2 minutes. Remove from the water and place in a bowl of really cold water.

Remove the asparagus from the water and dry off on kitchen roll. Rub the asparagus with the oil and place in the grill-pan and cook for 1 minute. Remove it from the heat and keep it warm.

And finally…

Place the butternut squash on to six large, warmed serving plates. Divide the wild mushroom risotto into six and place it in the centre of the butternut squash.

Place a spear of asparagus over the risotto and set some of the shaved Parmesan on top of the asparagus. Break the pumpkin seed biscuit into six equal pieces and push one biscuit into the top of each piece of butternut squash. Spoon the sauce over and around the squash and serve.

Goat's Cheese Spring Rolls
with Smoked Paprika Sauce

A delicious, contemporary dish that's been a huge success at The NEC...

Goat's Cheese Spring Rolls

320g goat's cheese

4 spring onions, finely chopped

8 sun-blushed tomatoes, finely chopped

Salt & pepper

2 egg yolks

½ tbsp water

6 sheets of spring roll pastry

25g sesame seeds

Goat's Cheese Spring Rolls

Pre-heat the deep-fat fryer to 180°C. Crumble the goat's cheese into a mixing bowl and add the spring onions and sun-blushed tomatoes. Season with salt & pepper and gently mix all the ingredients together. Place in the fridge.

Take a piece of spring roll pastry and cut into 20cm x 10cm strips. Place 1 tbsp of the goat's cheese mix at one end of each pastry strip and lay it down, leaving 1cm of pastry at either side.

Mix together the egg yolks and water. Brush all the sides of the pastry with egg wash and roll the pastry half-way up. Fold over the sides, brush the folded sides and top of the pastry with more egg wash and continue rolling so the ends become sealed and the spring rolls resemble those in the picture. Brush one side of the spring rolls with the egg wash and sprinkle them with the sesame seeds. Deep-fry them in the hot oil for 4 minutes until golden brown. Keep them warm.

Fondant Potato

6 medium baking potatoes, peeled
40g salted butter
1 tbsp vegetable oil
1 litre vegetable stock (see page 207)
Pinch of saffron
Salt & pepper

Fondant Potato

Pre-heat the oven to 150°C. Using a 5cm stainless steel round cutter, cut the potatoes into six cylinder shapes. Remove the excess potato from each end. Melt half the butter in a non-stick frying pan and add the oil. Brown one end of each potato. Place the potatoes in a deep roasting tin (approximately 30cm x 20cm) browned side up. Bring the vegetable stock to the boil and pour over the potatoes, leaving the top 1cm of the potatoes uncovered. Add the saffron, the rest of the butter and some salt & pepper. Place the roasting tin in the oven for 1 hour until the potatoes are cooked. Remove from the oven but leave the potatoes in the stock so they remain warm.

Smoked Paprika Sauce

½ tbsp olive oil
1 shallot, finely chopped
1 clove of garlic, finely chopped
1 tsp smoked paprika
2 tbsp white wine
1 tbsp tomato purée
1 red pepper, chopped
Sprig of tarragon
250g plum tomatoes
½ litre vegetable stock (see page 207)
Salt & pepper

Smoked Paprika Sauce

Heat the olive oil in a small saucepan and gently fry the shallot and garlic with the paprika for 1 minute until soft. Add the wine and cook for 1 minute. Add the tomato purée, pepper, tarragon, tomatoes and vegetable stock and bring to the boil. Season with salt & pepper and simmer for 20 minutes. Using a hand blender, whizz the sauce until it's smooth, then pass it through a fine sieve into a clean saucepan and keep it warm.

Vegetable Garnish

1 large leek
4 tbsp olive oil
1 aubergine
1 large red pepper, de-seeded and cut
  into 6
170g fine green beans
Salt & pepper

Vegetable Garnish

Pre-heat a grill pan. Slice the white part of the leek at a 45° angle, as shown in the photograph. Pour the olive oil into a bowl and dip the leeks into it. Remove any excess oil and place the leeks in the grill pan and cook for 1 minute on each side. Remove from the pan and keep them warm.

Slice the aubergines lengthways, 1cm thick, and brush them in the olive oil before cooking them in the grill pan for 2 minutes on each side. Remove them from the pan and slice them in half lengthways. Set them aside and ensure they stay warm.

Brush the peppers with olive oil and cook them in the grill pan for 2 minutes on both sides. Remove them from the pan and keep them warm.

Bring a medium saucepan of salted water to the boil. Add the green beans and cook for 2 minutes, then remove from the water and keep them warm.

And finally…

Salt & pepper

And finally…

Place the fondant potatoes on six large, warm serving plates. Lay the aubergines, green beans, peppers and char-grilled leeks in the centre of the plate and season.

Take a chopstick and skewer one of the spring rolls lengthways. Lay one spring roll on top of the vegetable garnish and set the skewered spring roll on top of the first. Spoon the sauce around the garnish and serve.

Porcini Mushroom Ravioli with Roasted Artichokes and Saffron Butter Sauce

This isn't a quick dish, but if you have time making pasta from scratch can be really relaxing and it tastes fantastic. Your guests will be hugely impressed that you've gone to all this trouble…

Fresh Pasta

300g pasta flour

3 large eggs

8 egg yolks

Porcini Ravioli Filling

160g dried Porcini mushrooms, soaked in water

1 tbsp olive oil

3 medium shallots, peeled and finely chopped

2 cloves of garlic, crushed

150ml white wine

600g ricotta cheese

Salt & pepper

1 tbsp chives, chopped

1 sprig of chervil, chopped

Fresh Pasta

Place the flour on a clean surface. Make a well in the centre and add all of the eggs and egg yolks. With a fork, break up the eggs as you bring in the flour then stir with the fork until you have a dough that you can work with your hands. Knead well until you have a smooth and elastic dough. Wrap the dough in clingfilm and leave in the fridge for at least 30 minutes.

Porcini Ravioli Filling

Strain off the mushrooms and dry them on kitchen roll. Roughly chop the mushrooms and leave to one side.

Place a large non-stick frying pan on the stove, heat the olive oil, add the shallots and garlic and gently sauté for 2 minutes, not allowing them to brown.

Add the mushrooms to the pan and cook for a further 2 minutes. Add the white wine and reduce by half; this should take around 3 minutes. Remove from the heat and empty into a bowl, then refrigerate the mix until chilled. When it's chilled, combine it with the ricotta cheese, the seasoning, chives and chervil and return to the fridge.

Making the Ravioli

Divide the pasta in two and keep the half you are not using covered. Working with one piece at a time, flatten it out with your hands, dust it with flour and put it through the thickest setting on a pasta machine. You can buy these from any cookware shop.

Then fold it in half and put it through the machine again. Repeat this process several times as it makes the pasta easier to work with. Continue lightly dusting the pasta with flour and move the settings lower each time, so the pasta will become thinner. You should put it through each setting twice, resting it between each rolling for about a minute. Do this until you have reached the desired thickness, which is around 2mm thick.

Take six 8cm ramekins and dust the inside with a little flour. Lay half the pasta on a floured work surface and cut out six large squares approximately 14cm x 14cm. Push the pasta into the ramekins, making sure there is at least a 2cm overhang of pasta outside of the ramekin.

Fill the ramekins equally with the ricotta mix, leaving a ½cm gap from the top. Take the rest of the pasta and cut into six 8cm squares. Brush one side liberally with egg yolk and press it down firmly on the top of the filled ramekin. Make sure there is no air caught inside.

Remove the ravioli from the ramekin and squeeze around the edge to make sure it is well sealed. Place the ravioli flat side down on a floured work surface, then place an 8cm pastry cutter over the top and cut away any excess pasta so it looks round and neat.

Place the ravioli in a pan of simmering water and cook for approximately 3 minutes. Lift gently out and keep them warm.

Saffron Butter Sauce

1 tbsp olive oil
1 large shallot, diced
100ml white wine
1 pinch saffron
350ml double cream
100g cold butter, diced small
1 tsp tarragon, finely chopped

Vegetable Garnish

18 baby carrots, peeled and cut in 3
12 baby leeks, cleaned and cut in 3
12 baby asparagus spears
150g sugar snap peas
100g broad beans, peeled
9 tinned artichoke hearts, cut in half
1 tbsp olive oil
150g wild mushrooms, cleaned & sliced
Salt & pepper

Saffron Butter Sauce

Heat the olive oil in a medium non-stick saucepan and cook the shallot for around 2 minutes. Don't allow it to brown. Pour in the white wine, add the saffron and reduce by half; this should take around 3 minutes.

Add the cream and gently heat until just simmering. Be careful not to boil the sauce as it will split. Lower the heat and gently add the diced butter to the pan, a little at a time, until the sauce begins to thicken. When all the butter has been added, put in the chopped tarragon, infuse for 5 minutes, pass through a fine sieve into a clean pan and keep the sauce warm.

Vegetable Garnish

Bring a pan of salted water to the boil. Add the carrots and cook for 2 minutes, then add the leeks, asparagus, sugar snap peas and broad beans and cook for a further minute. Drain, season and keep them warm.

Heat a large non-stick frying pan on the stove until smoking. Place the artichokes in the pan, cut side down, and heat until dark brown on the flat side. Remove from the pan and keep them warm. Place the pan back on the stove and heat the olive oil. Fry the mushrooms for 2 minutes, season, then remove them from the pan and keep them warm.

And finally...

Place the ravioli at the centre of six large warm serving plates or bowls. Divide the mushrooms into six and place a pile on top of each ravioli. Place three artichoke halves around the ravioli, divide the rest of the garnish into six and place it in between the artichokes and around the ravioli. Set two pieces of asparagus on top of the mushrooms, spoon the saffron sauce over and around the ravioli and serve.

Roasted Wild Mushrooms with Red Cabbage, Lavender Potatoes, Baby Vegetables and a Pumpkin Sauce

This recipe shows just how interesting vegetarian food can be...

Lavender Anna Potato

1.5kg Maris Piper potatoes
Salt & pepper
1 small sprig fresh lavender, finely chopped
200g melted butter

Lavender Anna Potato

Pre-heat the oven to 160°C. Slice the potatoes thinly and evenly on a mandolin. Place in a colander and liberally sprinkle with salt & pepper, leave to one side for 5 minutes to drain any of the excess water out.

Remove from the colander and dry off on kitchen roll. Sprinkle the lavender over the potatoes. Layer the potatoes neatly in six 10cm tartlet tins until the mould is well filled. The first layer in the tin will be the presentation side, so make sure you arrange it as neatly as possible.

Pour the butter equally over the top of the potatoes, place in the oven and cook for 40-45 minutes until golden brown. Remove from the oven and keep warm.

Red Cabbage

1 medium red cabbage
3 red apples
150g redcurrant jelly
150g Demerara sugar
1 cinnamon stick, broken in half
150ml Port wine

Red Cabbage

Pre-heat the oven to 140°C. Peel off the top leaves of the cabbage and discard them. Cut the cabbage into quarters remove the core and slice thinly. Core and dice the apples. Place all the ingredients into a suitably sized ovenproof container with a tight-fitting lid and cook in the oven for 1 hour, stirring every 15 minutes and checking that it's not catching. If it is, add a couple of tablespoons of water.

Drain the cabbage into a colander catching the liquor in a saucepan. Bring the liquid to the boil and reduce by half, add the liquor back to the cabbage and keep it warm.

Pumpkin Sauce

1 tbsp olive oil
100g shallots, peeled and finely chopped
280g pumpkin
½ litre vegetable stock (see page 207)
Salt & pepper

Mushroom Garnish

2 tbsp olive oil
200g wild mushrooms, cleaned and sliced
Salt & pepper
50g Portobello mushrooms, sliced thickly,
  lengthways

Vegetable Garnish

18 baby carrots, peeled and cut in half
6 baby leeks, cut in half
125g baby asparagus, cut in half, woody
  end removed
125g fine green beans, topped and tailed
25g butter
Salt & pepper

Pumpkin Sauce

Heat the olive oil in a medium saucepan and gently cook the shallots for 3 minutes, not allowing them to brown. Peel, chop and de-seed the pumpkin. Add the pumpkin and cook for a further 3 minutes. Pour in the vegetable stock, bring to the boil and simmer for 10 minutes. Remove from the heat and, using a hand blender, blend the mix until smooth. Pass through a fine strainer into a clean saucepan, season and keep warm. If the sauce appears too thick, add a little water to thin it down.

Mushroom Garnish

Heat the 1 tbsp of olive oil in a non-stick frying pan and cook the wild mushrooms for 2 minutes. Season with salt & pepper and drain on kitchen roll. Return the pan to the stove and add another tbsp of olive oil. Add the Portobello mushrooms to the pan and cook on both sides for 1 minute until golden brown. Remove from the pan and put them with the wild mushrooms and keep them warm.

Vegetable Garnish

Bring a medium saucepan of salted water to the boil. Cook the carrots for 2 minutes, then add the rest of the vegetables and cook for a further 2 minutes. Drain through a colander and put the vegetables back into the saucepan. Melt the butter over the vegetables. Season and keep them warm.

And finally…

Place an Anna potato on six large, warm serving plates and place a spoonful of the red cabbage on top. Set the wild mushrooms on top of the cabbage with a slice of Portobello mushroom on top. Place a pile of the vegetable garnish in front of the potato and spoon the sauce on either side of the potato and vegetable garnish.

Wild Mushroom Risotto with Shaved Pecorino and Basil Olive Oil

This is such a renowned and comforting dish, which is perfect as a starter or a main course. Simply adjust the amounts accordingly…

Wild Mushroom Risotto

2 tbsp olive oil

2 shallots, peeled and finely chopped

2 cloves of garlic, finely chopped

300g risotto rice (eg Arborio)

150ml white wine

1 litre vegetable stock (see page 207)

150g wild mushrooms, cleaned

100g button mushrooms

40g butter

125g baby asparagus

350g shaved Pecorino

1 tbsp chives, finely chopped

1 tbsp parsley, chopped

Salt & pepper

Wild Mushroom Risotto

Heat a medium saucepan on the stove. Add 1 tbsp of olive oil, the shallots and garlic and cook over a medium heat for 1 minute, not allowing them to brown. Add the rice and cook for a minute, stirring continuously until the rice becomes opaque.

Add the white wine and cook for a further minute until the wine is completely absorbed. Gradually add the stock to the rice, stirring all the time, until all the stock has been used. This should take 12-15 minutes and the rice should have a slight bite.

In a separate non-stick frying pan, heat the remaining olive oil, then add the mushrooms and asparagus and gently sauté them off for 3 minutes.

To finish, take half the mushrooms, asparagus and Pecorino and all of the butter, chives and parsley and stir into the risotto. Keep the remaining mushrooms, asparagus and Pecorino for garnishing. Season with salt & pepper and keep it warm.

Basil Oil

1 bunch fresh picked basil

1 bunch fresh chives

150ml extra-virgin olive oil

Salt & pepper

Basil Oil

Place all the ingredients in a blender and whizz for exactly 2 minutes until the oil is bright green. Do not over-blend as it will turn the oil a brownish-green. Season according to taste, then pass through a fine strainer and transfer to a squeezy bottle.

And finally…

Divide the risotto mix equally between six large, warm serving bowls. Set the remaining mushrooms, asparagus and Pecorino on top of the risotto. Drizzle over a little of the basil oil and serve.

With the support and inspiration of The NEC Group team I've been able to achieve my goals.

John Berry
Pastry Chef, The NEC Group
Four-time gold medal winner, World Culinary Olympics
Sixteen-time gold medal winner at Les Salons Culinaires (British Cookery Championships)

Nougatine Ice Cream
with Orange Snap and Coulis

This refreshing pudding looks amazing and tastes just as good...

Nougatine

150g caster sugar

50ml water

50g hazelnuts, chopped

50g peeled pistachios, chopped

Nougatine

Put the sugar and water into a medium saucepan and heat for 10 minutes until a light coloured caramel forms. Remove from the heat and pour on to a non-stick baking sheet. Sprinkle the hazelnuts and pistachios on top of the caramel and leave to cool down. When the caramel is cold, break it into small pieces and crush it with a rolling pin.

Ice Cream

500ml milk

250g caster sugar

8 egg yolks

300ml semi-whipped cream

Ice Cream

Place the milk in a medium saucepan and bring to the boil. Remove from the heat. Whisk the sugar and egg yolks in a large stainless steel mixing bowl until they're light and fluffy. Pour the hot milk on to the mix and whisk thoroughly. Place the bowl on top of a pan of boiling water and stir consistently with a wooden spoon until the mix starts to thicken and coat the back of the spoon. Remove immediately from the heat and pour through a fine sieve into a clean bowl. Leave the mix to cool. Add the cream. Pour into an ice cream machine and churn. When the ice cream is starting to set, add the crushed nougatine and then continue to churn until it is set. Pour into a rectangular container and place in the freezer for 24 hours.

Orange Snap

50g butter
50g caster sugar
1 orange, juiced
1 tbsp orange liqueur
25g plain flour

Orange Snap

Pre-heat the oven to 160°C. Cream the butter and sugar together in a medium mixing bowl. Add the wet ingredients, interspersing with the flour, and mix into a thick paste. Spread the mix on to a non-stick baking sheet roughly 8cm in diameter by 2 mm thick. Bake in the oven for 5 minutes until golden brown. Remove from the oven and allow to cool down on the tray, before carefully lifting off.

Orange Syrup

225g caster sugar
300ml water
1 orange, chopped

Orange Syrup

Place the sugar, water and chopped orange in a medium saucepan and place on a medium heat for 30 minutes until the mixture takes on a syrupy consistency. Drain through a fine strainer into a squeezy bottle, allow to cool and keep to one side.

Fruit Garnish

6 small apricots
2 oranges
Icing sugar for dredging

Fruit Garnish

Slice the apricots in half and remove the stone. Peel the orange, remove any pith and cut out each of the segments. Place the apricots, cut side up, and the orange segments on to a medium baking tray and cover them liberally with icing sugar. Using a blowtorch, caramelise the top of the fruit until golden brown.

And finally...

6 raspberries
6 mint sprigs

And finally...

Remove the ice cream from the freezer and leave for 5 minutes so it is easier to slice. Remove it from the tin and slice it into six equal bricks roughly 5cm wide, 10cm long and 5cm deep.

Place the ice cream on six serving plates and lay the orange snap biscuit on top of the ice cream. Place two of the glazed apricots, oranges and raspberries on top of the ice cream and a piece of the picked mint as pictured and spoon the sauce around the ice cream.

Zabaglione Red Fruit Trifle with Meringue and Amaretti

With real visual impact and great flavours, this is a stunning finale to any dinner party...

Red Berry Coulis

200g raspberries
300g strawberries
150g caster sugar
100ml water

Red Berry Coulis

Place all the ingredients in a medium saucepan. Bring to the boil and cook for 4 minutes. Leave to cool for 5 minutes, then transfer to a blender and blitz for 3 minutes. Pass the sauce through a fine sieve and transfer to a squeezy bottle.

Meringue

2 eggs whites
125g caster sugar

Meringue

Pre-heat the oven to 120°C. Place the egg whites in a large mixing bowl and whisk them – adding the sugar a little at a time – until they start to form stiff peaks. Line a flat baking tray with parchment paper. Fill a piping bag with the meringue mixture and pipe out six long pointed triangle shapes 8cm long by 1cm deep as the picture shows. Cook in the oven for 1-1 ½ hours. Turn off the oven and allow the meringue to cool down in the oven with the door closed.

Zabaglione Mix

500g mascarpone
600ml double cream
4 tbsp icing sugar
50ml sherry

Zabaglione Mix

Mix all the ingredients together in a large mixing bowl and whisk until they become thicker, then place the mix in a piping bag with a small plain nozzle.

And finally…

200g raspberries
200g strawberries, cut into quarters
100g blueberries
1 fig
100g amaretti biscuits, lightly crushed
1 tbsp cocoa powder for dusting
6 mint sprigs
6 chocolate scrolls (can be purchased
   from a cake decorating shop)

And finally…

Take six large trifle glasses and place some of the crushed amaretti biscuits at the bottom. Place 2-3 raspberries, a few pieces of strawberry, 3 blueberries and 1 tablespoon of the coulis at the bottom of the glass. Pipe in a thin layer of the zabaglione mix on top of the fruit. Repeat the process five times until the whole glass is filled. Arrange the berries on top of the trifle as pictured. Cut the fig into six pieces and place it next to the berries. Set the meringue to the rear of the glass and stick a chocolate scroll through the centre. Set a piece of meringue and amaretti biscuit to the front. Finish the dish with a sprig of mint and a dusting of cocoa powder and serve.

Pear Tart with Gingerbread Ice Cream

Nothings beats classic pear tart and the gingerbread ice cream adds another delicious dimension...

Pastry

225g plain flour

Pinch of salt

1 lemon, zested

150g soft butter

25g caster sugar

1 egg yolk

1 whole egg

Flour for dusting

1 large bag of baking beans
  (to fill six 10cm circles)

Pastry

Rub the flour, salt, lemon zest and butter together with your fingers, until the mix resembles breadcrumbs. Add the sugar and slowly add the egg yolk and whole egg and continue to mix until you have a pastry dough. Transfer to a clean bowl, cover with clingfilm and refrigerate for 2 hours.

Pre-heat the oven to 170°C. Lightly flour a clean work surface and roll out the pastry until it's 3mm thick and cut into six 10cm circles. Take six, 8cm individual tart cases and lay a piece of pastry over the top of each. Carefully push the pastry inside the ring ensuring it doesn't tear. Fold the overhang of pastry back over into the ring and squeeze it around the edge to give a double thickness. Shape the pastry so it just rises over the edge of the ring.

Cover the pastry with a sheet of parchment paper and fill it with baking beans. Place the pastry cases in the oven and bake it blind in the oven for 10 minutes. Remove the pastry cases from the oven, carefully lift the parchment paper and beans out of the ring and return the pastry cases to the oven and cook for a further 5 minutes until golden brown. Remove the pastry cases from the oven and allow to cool.

Frangipane

150g butter
150g sugar
2 eggs
25g plain flour
150g ground almonds

Toffee Sauce

50g butter
150g Demerara sugar
2 tbsp golden syrup
50ml double cream

Gingerbread

125g plain flour
1 tsp ground ginger
1 tsp mixed spice
1 tsp bicarbonate of soda
25g soft sugar
50g butter
80g black treacle
25g golden syrup
60ml milk
1 egg, beaten

Poached Pears

6 William pears
Lemon juice
2 pints water
400g caster sugar
1 cinnamon stick

Frangipane

Cream the butter and sugar in a medium mixing bowl. Add the eggs and mix to a paste. Place the flour and almonds into the mix a little at a time until it has all been added.

Toffee Sauce

Place all the ingredients, except the cream, in a medium saucepan and bring to the boil. Simmer for 20 minutes. Remove the pan from the heat, leave the sauce to cool and stir in the cream.

Gingerbread

Pre-heat the oven to 160°C and grease an 18cm cake tin. In a large mixing bowl, mix the flour, ginger, mixed spice, bicarbonate of soda and sugar together.

Gently heat the butter, treacle and syrup in a small saucepan. Gradually add the milk. Remove the pan from the heat and allow to cool. When the mix has cooled, add the egg and stir in the flour. Pour the cake mix into the tin and bake in the oven for 30 minutes or until it's firm. Remove from the oven and allow to cool on a wire rack. Cut the gingerbread into 1cm dice and leave to one side to use in the ice cream later.

Poached Pears

Peel the pears and place them in a bowl of water with a little lemon juice to stop them discolouring. Place the water, sugar and cinnamon in a medium saucepan and bring to the boil. Reduce to a simmer and put in the pears. Cook them for 40 minutes until they're tender. Remove the pan from the heat and allow the pears to cool down in the liquid.

Ice Cream

500ml milk

250g caster sugar

8 egg yolks

300ml semi-whipped cream

Ice Cream

Pour the milk into a medium saucepan and bring to the boil. Remove the pan from the heat. Whisk the sugar and egg yolks in a large stainless steel mixing bowl until you have a light and fluffy mixture. Pour the hot milk into the mix and whisk thoroughly. Place the bowl on top of a pan of boiling water and stir consistently with a wooden spoon until the mix starts to thicken and coat the back of the spoon. Remove the pan from the heat and pour the mix through a fine sieve into a clean bowl.

Leave the mixture to cool. Add the whipped cream. Pour the ice cream mix into an ice cream machine and churn. When it's almost set, add the diced gingerbread mix for 30 seconds and turn off the machine, so you don't break up the gingerbread too much. Remove the ice cream, put it into a suitable container with a lid and place in the freezer.

Toffee Biscuit

25g golden syrup

25g butter

75g caster sugar

25g plain flour

Toffee Biscuit

Pre-heat the oven to 180°C. Place the syrup, butter and sugar into a medium saucepan and stir over a low heat until the sugar has dissolved. Remove the pan from the heat and stir in the flour. Leave the mix to one side to cool down for 1 hour. Drop six teaspoons of mix on to a non-stick baking sheet, roughly 5cm apart from each other.

Bake in the oven for approximately 7-10 minutes or until golden brown. Remove the biscuits from the oven and leave to cool on the tray.

And finally…

Place a spoonful of the toffee sauce at the centre of six large serving plates. Place the tart on top of the sauce and set the poached pear at the centre of the tart. Make an incision in the pear and slide in the toffee biscuit. Ball the gingerbread ice cream and set it next to the tart.

Chocolate Truffle with Mango Rice Conde and Pistachio Ice Cream

This delightful pudding is well worth a little time and effort as your guests will love it...

Pistachio Ice Cream

500ml milk

250g caster sugar

8 egg yolks

300ml semi-whipped cream

100g peeled pistachios,
  chopped

Pistachio Ice Cream

Place the milk in a medium saucepan and bring to the boil. Remove from the heat. Whisk the sugar and egg yolks in a large stainless steel mixing bowl until they're light and fluffy.

Pour the hot milk on to the mix and whisk thoroughly. Place the bowl on top of a pan of boiling water and stir consistently with a wooden spoon until the mix starts to thicken and coat the back of the spoon. Remove immediately from the heat and pour through a fine sieve into a clean bowl. Leave the mix to cool.

Add the cream. Pour into an ice cream machine and churn. When the ice cream is starting to set, add the pistachios and churn the ice cream until it is set. Pour into a suitable container and place in the freezer.

Chocolate Truffle

150g dark chocolate

33ml warm water

33g golden syrup

1 tbsp rum

15g powdered gelatine

200ml whipping cream

Cocoa for dusting

Chocolate Truffle

Break the chocolate into small even pieces and place them in a bowl. Bring a saucepan of water to the boil, simmer and place the bowl of chocolate on top to melt stirring occasionally. Put the warm water, syrup, rum and gelatine into a medium saucepan and gently heat for 5 minutes, then add the melted chocolate to the rum mix. Whip the cream until it reaches soft peaks and then gently fold in the mixed chocolate and rum.

Take six 5cm stainless steel rings, grease the inside of them with a little oil and cut the sponge out to fit in the bottom. Place the rings on a tray and then spoon the truffle mix into them, making sure there are no air pockets inside. Lightly dust the tops with cocoa powder and place the tray in the fridge for 2-3 hours until firm (preferably overnight).

Red Berry Coulis

200g raspberries

300g strawberries

150g caster sugar

100ml water

Mango Coulis

3 mangoes, peeled and diced

150g caster sugar

100ml water

Meringue

2 egg whites

110g caster sugar

Biscotti

125g plain flour

125g caster sugar

½ tbsp baking powder

25g sultanas

25g white chocolate, finely chopped

25g dark chocolate, finely chopped

25g peeled pistachios

25g hazelnuts

3 eggs

Red Berry Coulis

Place all the ingredients in a medium saucepan, bring them to the boil and cook for 4 minutes. When the mix has been left to cool down for 5 minutes, transfer it to a blender and blitz for 3 minutes. Pass it through a fine sieve and transfer to a squeezy bottle.

Mango Coulis

Place all the ingredients in a medium saucepan. Bring them to the boil and cook for 4 minutes. When the mix has been left to cool down for 5 minutes, transfer it to a blender and blitz for 3 minutes. Pass it through a fine sieve and transfer to a squeezy bottle.

Meringue

Pre-heat the oven to 120°C. Place the egg whites in a large mixing bowl and whisk them, while adding the sugar a little at a time, until they start to form stiff peaks. Fill a piping bag with the meringue mix and pipe out six long, pointed triangle shapes 8cm long by 1cm deep on to a non-stick baking sheet. Cook in the oven for 1-1½ hours. Turn off the oven and allow the meringue to cool down in the oven with the door closed.

Biscotti

Pre-heat the oven to 160°C. Place all the ingredients in a bowl, with the eggs going in last, and mix until you have a dough. Place the dough on to a non-stick baking sheet. Flatten the dough out so it is roughly 2cm thick and 12cm wide. Bake in the oven for 30 minutes until it's firm. Remove from the oven and cut the biscotti into thin slices. Place the cut biscotti back on the baking sheet and cook for a further 10 minutes until they're hard.

Rice Conde

50g short-grain rice
500ml milk
1 vanilla pod, split
25g caster sugar

And finally…

120g crunchy nut muesli, chopped
12 blueberries for garnishing
12 redcurrants for garnishing
12 raspberries
6 mint sprigs

Rice Conde

Place the rice, milk and vanilla pod in a medium heatproof bowl and put on top of a double boiler. Cover and cook for 40 minutes until the rice has absorbed the milk and become thick and creamy. Remove the rice from the bowl, mix in the sugar and place in the fridge for 20 minutes.

And finally…

Take six large fluted shot glasses and pour 1 teaspoon of mango coulis into the bottom, then fill the glass up to one third with rice. Pour 1 teaspoon of the red berry coulis on top of the rice and then fill up with the remaining rice, leaving a 5mm gap at the top.

Pour 1 teaspoon of mango coulis on to the rice and to sprinkle on the muesli. Spike the top of the conde with a piece of the meringue and biscotti and then set the berries on top.

Place the shot glass of rice at the top of six large serving plates, set the chocolate truffle next to it and gently remove the metal ring. Spoon 1 teaspoon of the raspberry coulis over the top of the truffle and place 2 raspberries on top with a sprig of mint.

Ball the ice cream and set it in between the shot glass and truffle and serve.

Apple, Cranberry and Walnut Muffins
with Vanilla Ice Cream and Caramelised Fruit

Fruity, nutty and sweet, this pudding is guaranteed to please...

Apple, Cranberry and Walnut Muffins

300g self-raising flour

150g brown sugar

150g cranberries

1 tsp mixed spice

2 Braeburn apples, cored
  and roughly diced

1 tsp ground cinnamon

50g walnuts, chopped

1 egg

175ml buttermilk

125ml vegetable oil

1 tbsp butter for greasing

Apple, Cranberry and Walnut Muffins

Pre-heat the oven to 170°C. Place all the dry ingredients in a large mixing bowl, stir in the remaining ingredients and mix until they are all combined. Spoon the mixture into a greased muffin tin or multiple paper cases. Place them in the oven for about 25 minutes or until cooked. Remove them from the oven and allow them to cool on a wire rack.

Caramelised Fruit

3 Braeburn apples

150g Demerara sugar

Caramelised Fruit

Core and cut the apples into six pieces. Heat the sugar in a pan with a little water until it melts and becomes a light caramel. Add the apple to the mix and roll them to coat them in the caramel for 5 minutes. Remove the caramelised apples from the pan and place them on a plate.

Toffee Sauce

50g butter

150g Demerara sugar

2 tbsp golden syrup

50ml double cream

Toffee Sauce

Put all the ingredients, except the cream, in a medium saucepan and bring to the boil. Simmer for 20 minutes. Remove the pan from the heat and leave the sauce to cool. Stir in the cream.

Vanilla Ice Cream

500ml milk

2 vanilla pods

250g caster sugar

8 egg yolks

300ml double cream,
  lightly whipped

Chocolate Curls

250g dark chocolate

And finally…

6 large strawberries, cut
  in half

6 mint sprigs

1 tbsp icing sugar, for dusting

Vanilla Ice Cream

Place the milk and vanilla pods in a medium saucepan. Bring to the boil and remove from the heat. Whisk the sugar and egg yolks in a large stainless steel mixing bowl until the mixture is light and fluffy. Pour the hot milk into the bowl and whisk thoroughly. Place the bowl on top of a pan of boiling water and stir continuously with a wooden spoon until the mix starts to thicken and coat the back of a wooden spoon. As soon as you've achieved this consistency, remove from the heat and pour through a fine sieve into a clean bowl. Leave the mixture to cool. Add the whipped cream, pour into an ice cream machine and churn until frozen. Remove the ice cream and place it in a suitable container with a lid and put it in the freezer.

Chocolate Curls

Break the chocolate into small, even-sized pieces and place them in a bowl. Bring a saucepan of water to the boil and then turn down the heat so the water simmers. Place the bowl of chocolate on top of the pan to melt the chocolate, stirring occasionally.

Remove the chocolate from the heat and pour a thin layer on to a non-stick baking sheet. Smooth the chocolate over with a palette knife and leave to one side to cool slightly so it becomes set. Roll it with a palette knife into six cigar shapes.

And finally…

Warm the muffins in the oven on a low heat for 5 minutes and remove them from the cases or tin. Place one towards the top of each of six serving plates. Take the caramelised apples and place three pieces on each of the plates with two strawberry halves. Take six balls of ice cream and place one next to each of the muffins and apples. Place a chocolate curl on top of the muffin. Drizzle the toffee sauce over the caramelised apples and finish with a sprig of mint and a light dusting of icing sugar.

Apple Sable and Caramelised Pecan Nuts with Toffee Sauce and Custard

The sweetness of the apple combines beautifully with the nutty flavours and the sinful toffee sauce and custard…

 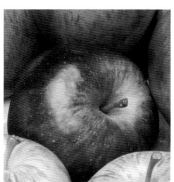

Apple Sable Mix

4 Bramley apples, peeled,
  cored and chopped
50g butter
150g Demerara sugar
¼ tsp cinnamon
30g sultanas
125g ground almonds
250g suet mix
450g plain flour
110ml water
1 tbsp vegetable oil
3 tbsp flour for dusting

Apple Sable Mix

Pre-heat the oven to 160°C. Place the apples in a medium saucepan, add the butter, sugar and cinnamon and cook over a medium heat for 10 minutes or until the apples are soft. Remove from the heat and mix in the sultanas and almonds.

Place the suet mix and plain flour in a medium mixing bowl and pour in the water. Mix well until the mixture comes together in the middle of the bowl and you have none sticking to the sides. Take six 8cm stainless steel rings and place them on a non-stick baking sheet, brushing the inside of the rings with the vegetable oil.

Flour a clean work surface and place the suet on it. Roll it out until it's 5mm thick and cut out six 20cm circles of suet paste. Gently push the suet paste into the rings, taking care not to rip or tear it, and pushing it evenly around the inside, leaving a 2cm overhang. Spoon the apple mix inside the rings, bring the sides of the suet to the centre and pinch together to break off any excess suet paste. Turn them over and place them back on to the non-stick baking sheet. Cook them in the oven for 30-40 minutes until golden brown. Remove from the oven and keep warm.

Apple Crisps

100g caster sugar

100ml water

2 Braeburn apples

Egg Custard Sauce

300ml milk

1 vanilla pod, split lengthways

6 egg yolks

150g caster sugar

Toffee Sauce

50g butter

150g Demerara sugar

2 tbsp golden syrup

50ml double cream

Caramelised Pecans

175g pecans

175g Demerara sugar

And finally…

18 blackberries for garnishing

1 tbsp icing sugar for dusting

Apple Crisps

Pre-heat the oven to 140°C. Mix 75g of the sugar with the water in a mixing bowl. Slice the apples 2mm thick and lay them on to a non-stick baking tray. Brush them with the sugar solution and sprinkle the remaining sugar mix on top. Bake in the oven for 20-30 minutes or until they're golden brown. Remove them from the oven and allow them to cool on the tray.

Egg Custard Sauce

Bring the milk and vanilla pod to the boil in a medium saucepan. Whisk the eggs and sugar together in a large mixing bowl and pour the milk over the sugar and eggs, whisking vigorously. Return the mixture back to the saucepan and heat gently – ensuring that it doesn't boil – until the mixture thickens slightly. Remove the pan from the heat, pour the mix through a fine sieve into a clean bowl and keep it warm.

Toffee Sauce

Place all the ingredients, except the cream, in a medium saucepan and bring to the boil. Simmer for 20 minutes. Remove from the heat and leave the sauce to cool. Stir in the cream.

Caramelised Pecans

Heat the sugar in a medium saucepan until it starts to melt and becomes a light caramel colour. Place the pecans in the sugar and stir until all are coated. Remove the pecans carefully from pan and place them on a non-stick baking sheet to cool down.

And finally…

Pour an equal amount of the egg custard sauce into the bottom of six large bowls. Place the warm apple sable on to the centre of the sauce and set the pecans on top of the sable. Spoon the toffee sauce over the top of the pecans and set two of the apple crisps on top of each. Place three of the blackberries around the bowl, then lightly dust with icing sugar and serve.

Chocolate Pear Tart with Chocolate Truffle and Vanilla Pod Custard

This is a must-try recipe for chocoholics everywhere…

Pastry

225g plain flour

Pinch of salt

1 lemon, zested

150g soft butter

25g caster sugar

1 egg yolk

1 whole egg

Flour for dusting

1 large bag of baking beans
  (to fill a 22cm flan tin)

Pastry

Rub the flour, salt, lemon zest and butter together with your fingers until the mix resembles breadcrumbs. Add the sugar, then slowly add the egg yolk and whole egg and continue to mix until you have a pastry dough. Transfer to a clean bowl, cover with clingfilm and refrigerate for 2 hours.

Pre-heat the oven to 180°C. Lightly flour a clean work surface and roll out the pastry until it's 3mm thick and 30cm wide. Take a 22cm flan tin and lay the pastry over the top. Carefully push the pastry inside the ring, making sure it doesn't tear. Fold the overhang of pastry back over into the ring and squeeze it around the edge to give a double thickness. Shape it so it just rises over the edge of the ring. Cover the pastry with a sheet of parchment paper and fill it with baking beans. Place the tin in the oven and bake it blind for 10 minutes. Remove the pastry from the oven, carefully lift the parchment paper and beans out of the ring, then return the pastry to the oven and cook for a further 5 minutes until it's golden brown. Remove the pastry from the oven and allow it to cool.

Poached Pears

6 William pears, peeled

Lemon juice

1.2 litres water

400g caster sugar

1 cinnamon stick

Poached Pears

Peel the pears and place them in a bowl of water with a little lemon juice to stop them discolouring. Place the water, sugar and cinnamon in a medium saucepan and bring to the boil. Reduce to a simmer and add the pears.

Cook them for 40 minutes until they're tender. Remove the pan from the heat and allow the pears to cool down in the liquid. Remove the pears and slice them in half lengthways. Using a melon baller or a teaspoon remove the pear core and leave the pears to one side until they're needed.

Tart Filling

225g dark chocolate
125g soft butter
125g caster sugar
3 eggs
125g ground almonds
25g plain flour
Poached pears from
 method on page 183
2 tbsp apricot jam

Tart Filling

Pre-heat the oven to 150°C. Break the chocolate into small even pieces and place them in a bowl. Bring a saucepan of water to the boil, simmer and place the bowl of chocolate on top to melt, stirring occasionally. Cream the butter and sugar together in a mixing bowl. Beat the eggs into the mixture, adding a little at a time, interspersing the almonds and flour a little at a time so as not to split the mixture. Beat the melted chocolate into the mix and spread a thin layer on to the bottom of the pastry case. Arrange the 12 pear halves, cut side down, on to the mix and spoon the remaining mix over and around the pears. Bake in the oven for 25-30 minutes. When the tart is cool, melt the apricot jam in a saucepan and brush it over the top to give it a glaze.

Sponge

4 eggs
2 egg yolks
125g caster sugar
100g flour, sifted
25g cocoa powder

Sponge

Pre-heat the oven to 160°C. Whisk all the eggs and sugar in a mixing bowl for 10 minutes until light and fluffy. Sift the flour and cocoa powder into the egg and sugar mix and gently fold them together. Smooth the mix over a non-stick baking sheet with a palette knife until it's 1cm thick. Bake in the oven for 5-10 minutes until it's firm. Remove the sponge from the oven and allow it to cool.

Chocolate Truffle

225g dark chocolate
50ml water
50g golden syrup
2 tbsp rum
15g powdered gelatine
300ml whipping cream
Cocoa for dusting

Chocolate Truffle

Break the chocolate into small even pieces and place them in a bowl. Bring a saucepan of water to the boil, simmer and place the bowl of chocolate on top to melt, stirring occasionally. Put the water, golden syrup, rum and gelatine into a medium saucepan and gently heat for 5 minutes, then add the melted chocolate to the rum mix. Whip the cream until it reaches soft peaks and then gently fold in the rum and chocolate mixture. Grease the inside of six 5cm stainless steel rings with a little oil. Cut out the sponge to fit in the bottom.

Place the rings on a tray and then spoon the truffle mix into them, making sure there are no air pockets inside. Lightly dust the tops with cocoa powder and place the tray in the fridge for 4-5 hours until they've firmed. It's preferable to do this overnight.

Egg Custard Sauce

200ml milk

1 vanilla pod, split lengthways

4 egg yolks

150g sugar

Bring the milk and the vanilla pod to the boil in a medium saucepan. Whisk the eggs and sugar together in a large mixing bowl and pour the milk over the sugar and eggs, whisking vigorously. Return the mix to the saucepan and gently heat – ensuring it doesn't boil – until the mixture thickens slightly. Remove the pan from the heat and pour the mix through a fine sieve into a clean bowl and allow it to cool down.

Ginger Snaps

25g butter

75g caster sugar

25g golden syrup

25g flour, sifted

½ tsp ground ginger

½ tsp lemon rind, grated

½ tsp lemon juice

Oil for greasing

Pre-heat the oven to 180°C. Place the butter, sugar and syrup in a medium saucepan and heat gently until the sugar has dissolved. Remove from the heat. Fold in the flour, ginger, lemon rind and lemon juice. Lightly grease two baking trays. Spoon 6 teaspoons of the mixture on to a non-stick baking sheet, leaving a 10cm gap between them. Bake for 7-10 minutes or until golden brown. Quickly remove the ginger snaps from the baking sheet using a palette knife and shape them around the handles of a wooden spoon while still hot. When they are set remove them from the wooden spoons and cool them on a wire rack. Repeat the process for the next five biscuits.

And finally

6 mint sprigs

Remove the tart gently from the ring and cut neatly into six slices and place one slice each on six plates. Gently push the chocolate truffles out of the moulds and set them to one side of the tart. Fill six large shot glasses with the egg custard sauce and place them between the tart and the truffle. Take the ginger snaps, lay them against the chocolate truffles and spike the top of the truffle with a sprig of mint.

Raspberry Kir Jelly with Mascarpone and Pistachio Tuille

This pudding is time-consuming but light, refreshing and tastes of summer. It is well worth the wait...

Sponge

4 eggs
2 egg yolks
125g caster sugar
100g flour, sifted
25g cocoa powder

Raspberry Kir Jelly

1 tbsp vegetable oil
1 tbsp icing sugar
6 x sponge disks
100ml water
40g gelatine powder
500ml crème de cassis
500ml champagne
375g fresh raspberries

Sponge

Pre-heat the oven to 160°C. Whisk the whole eggs, egg yolks and sugar in a mixing bowl for 10 minutes until they're light and fluffy. Sift the flour and cocoa into the eggs and sugar and gently fold them together. Place a non-stick baking sheet on a flat baking tray and smooth the mix over the top with a pallet knife until it's 1cm thick. Bake in the oven for 5-10 minutes until firm. Remove the sponge from the oven and allow to cool. Cut the moulds into six with 7cm stainless steel rings.

Raspberry Kir Jelly

Take six 7cm stainless steel pastry rings and brush the insides with the vegetable oil. Place the icing sugar in a sieve and sprinkle the inside of the moulds so they are completely covered. Place a sponge disk in the bottom of each of the rings; place them on a baking tray and put them in the freezer for 2 hours.

Place the water, gelatine, crème de cassis and champagne in a medium saucepan and heat gently, ensuring you don't allow it to boil. Remove from the heat and allow to cool down to room temperature.

Remove the moulds from the freezer and lay half of the raspberries on the sponge disk as the picture shows. Pour the jelly until it reaches half way up each mould just covering the raspberries. Return the mould to the fridge for 4-5 hours, or preferably overnight until the jelly is set. Take the jelly moulds and lay the remaining raspberries on top of the set jelly. Warm the remaining jelly in a saucepan until it becomes liquid. Pour up to the edge of the mould completely covering the second layer of raspberries and set in the fridge overnight.

Pistachio Tuille

50g butter

50g caster sugar

1 egg white

50g plain flour

40g peeled pistachios, chopped

Pistachio Tuille

Pre-heat the oven to 160°C. Cream the butter and sugar together in a medium mixing bowl, and the egg white and flour and mix until you have a smooth paste. Place a non-stick baking sheet on a flat baking tray and spread a teaspoon of the mix thinly over the paper roughly 6cm in diameter, then repeat until you have six tuilles pasted on to the paper.

Sprinkle on the chopped pistachios and bake in the oven for 5 minutes or until they're golden brown. Remove from the oven and allow the tuilles to cool on the tray.

Egg Custard Sauce

150ml milk

1 vanilla pod, split lengthways

3 egg yolks

125g caster sugar

Egg Custard Sauce

Bring the milk to the boil in a medium saucepan with the vanilla pod. Whisk the eggs and sugar together in a large mixing bowl and pour the milk over them while whisking vigorously. Return the mix back to the saucepan and gently heat, ensuring it doesn't boil, until the mixture thickens slightly. Remove the pan from the heat and pour the mix through a fine sieve into a clean bowl to cool.

And finally…

150g Mascarpone, for garnishing

6 sprigs of mint

70g raspberries

And finally…

Take the jelly out of the fridge, leave to one side for 10 minutes, then carefully remove it from the mould. Place the jelly in the middle of the plate and place a shaped teaspoon of Mascarpone on to one side of the jelly. Set three of the remaining raspberries on top of each of the jellies and stud a piece of mint into the mascarpone.

Finish the dish with a tablespoon of egg custard sauce at the front of the plate and put a tuille into the Mascarpone as shown.

Two-nut Tart with Pistachio Ice Cream and Espresso Custard

You'll love the coffee-infused custard – so deliciously decadent...

Pastry

225g plain flour
Pinch of salt
1 lemon, zested
150g soft butter
25g caster sugar
1 egg yolk
1 whole egg
Flour for dusting
1 large bag of baking beans

Pastry

Rub the flour, salt, lemon zest and butter together with your fingers until the mix resembles breadcrumbs. Add the sugar and slowly add the egg yolk and then 1 whole egg and continue to mix until you have a pastry dough. Transfer to a clean bowl, cover with clingfilm and refrigerate for 2 hours.

Pre heat the oven to 170°C. Lightly flour a clean work surface and roll the pastry out until it's 3mm thick and cut into six pieces. Take six 8cm individual tart cases and lay a piece of pastry over the top of each. Carefully push the pastry inside the ring, ensuring it doesn't tear. Fold the overhang of pastry back over into the ring and squeeze it around the edge to give a double thickness. Shape the pastry so it rises just over the edge of the ring.

Cover the pastry with a sheet of greaseproof paper and fill it with baking beans. Place the pastry cases in the oven and bake blind for 10 minutes. Remove the pastry cases from the oven, then carefully lift the greaseproof paper and beans out of the ring and return the pastry cases to the oven and cook for a further 5 minutes until they're golden brown. Remove the pastry cases from the oven and allow them to cool.

Filling

25g caster sugar
65g butter
2 eggs, separated
75g dark chocolate, finely grated
½ tbsp cocoa powder
50g walnuts, finely chopped
50g almonds, finely chopped

Filling

Pre-heat the oven to 160°C. Beat the sugar and butter together in a large bowl until the mixture is light in colour. Mix in the egg yolks until the mixture becomes thick and creamy. Whisk the egg whites until they become stiff. Stir the chocolate, cocoa powder, walnuts and almonds into the mixture and then gently fold in the egg whites. Spoon the mix into the pastry cases and bake in the oven for 20 minutes until the filling becomes firm.

Ice Cream

500ml milk

250g caster sugar

8 egg yolks

300ml semi-whipped cream

100g pistachios, chopped

Ice Cream

Place the milk in a medium saucepan. Bring to the boil and remove from the heat. Whisk the sugar and egg yolks in a large stainless steel mixing bowl until they're light and fluffy. Pour the hot milk on to the mix and whisk thoroughly.

Place the bowl on top of a pan of boiling water and stir with a wooden spoon until the mix starts to thicken and coats the back of the spoon. Remove immediately from the heat and pour through a fine sieve into a clean bowl. Leave the mix to cool.

Add the cream, pour into an ice cream maker and churn. When the ice cream is starting to set add the pistachios and churn the ice cream until set. Then pour in a suitable container and place in the freezer.

Nutty Florentine

50g caster sugar

1 egg white

50g plain flour

25g pistachios, chopped

25g pecan nuts, sliced

Nutty Florentine

Pre-heat the oven to 160°C. Cream the butter and sugar together in a medium mixing bowl, add the egg white and flour and mix until you have a smooth paste.

Spread a teaspoon of the mix on a non-stick baking sheet until it's roughly 6cm in diameter. Repeat until you have six Florentines on the paper. Sprinkle on the pistachios and pecans and bake in the oven for 5 minutes or until they're golden brown. Remove them from the oven and allow the Florentines to cool down on the tray.

Espresso Custard

50g Camp coffee
150ml milk
3 egg yolks
125g caster sugar

Chocolate Curls

150g dark chocolate

Espresso Custard

Pour the coffee and milk into a medium saucepan and bring to the boil. Whisk the eggs and sugar together in a large mixing bowl and pour the milk over the sugar and egg yolks whisking vigorously. Return the mix back to the saucepan and gently heat – ensuring that it doesn't boil – until the mixture thickens slightly. Remove the pan from the heat and pour the mix through a fine sieve into a clean bowl to cool down. Transfer to a clean container and place in the fridge.

Chocolate Curls

Break the chocolate into small even pieces and place them in a bowl. Bring a saucepan of water to the boil, simmer and place the bowl of chocolate on top to melt. Pour the chocolate on to a smooth flat surface, such as the back of a large flat baking tray. Leave to set, then place the edge of a palette knife on the top of the chocolate and, pulling towards you, scrape off the chocolate curls.

And finally…

Place one tart at the centre of each of the six large serving plates. Spoon the sauce around the tart and place a ball of the ice cream on top of the tart. Make a small incision in the top of the ice cream and slot in the Florentine. Place a chocolate curl on top of the tart and serve.

Passion Fruit Tart with Chocolate Mascarpone

This is a delight to share – your guests will love its sweet and tart mix...

Pastry

225g plain flour

Pinch of salt

1 lemon, zested

150g soft butter

25g caster sugar

1 egg yolk

1 whole egg

1 large bag of baking beans
  (to fill a 20cm flan ring)

Pastry

Rub the flour, salt, lemon zest and butter together until the mix resembles breadcrumbs. Add the sugar and slowly add the egg yolk and whole egg and continue to mix until you have a pastry dough. Transfer to a bowl, cover with clingfilm and refrigerate for two hours.

Pre-heat the oven to 170°C. Lightly flour a work surface and roll the pastry out 3mm thick and 25cm wide. Take a 20cm flan ring and lay the pastry over the top. Carefully push the pastry inside the ring, making sure not to tear it. Fold over the overhang of pastry back over into the ring and squeeze it around the edge to give a double thickness. Shape the pastry so it just rises over the edge of the ring.

Cover the pastry with a sheet of parchment paper and fill it with baking beans. Place the pastry in the oven and bake it blind in the oven for 10 minutes. Remove the pastry from the oven, carefully lift the parchment paper and beans out of the ring and return the pastry to the oven. Cook for a further 5 minutes until golden brown. Remove the pastry from the oven and allow it to cool.

Passion Fruit Filling

275g double cream

6 eggs

200g caster sugar

3 passion fruit, seeds sieved out

2 tbsp icing sugar for dusting

Passion Fruit Filling

Pre-heat the oven to 160°C. Mix the cream, eggs, sugar and the passion fruit pulp in a large mixing bowl and pour into the pastry case, leaving a 2mm gap at the top. Bake in the oven for 30 minutes until set. The centre of the tart should have a slight wobble to it. Dust the top with icing sugar and glaze until golden brown with a blowtorch.

Passion Fruit Syrup

150g caster sugar

300ml water

Pulp of 2 passion fruit

Glazed Pineapple

1 small pineapple

1 tbsp icing sugar for glazing

Chocolate Mascarpone

200g mascarpone

40g dark chocolate

And finally...

6 sprigs of mint

6 raspberries

6 chocolate scrolls
 (can be purchased from a
 cake decorating shop)

Passion Fruit Syrup

Place all the ingredients in a medium saucepan and bring to the boil. Simmer for 30 minutes until the syrup starts to thicken. Remove from the heat and leave to cool.

Glazed Pineapple

Peel off the skin from the pineapple and cut it in half lengthways. Cut into quarters and remove the core. Slice the pineapple into 12 x 1cm thick pieces and place on a baking tray, then dust the pineapple with icing sugar and caramelise with a blowtorch until golden brown.

Chocolate Mascarpone

Grate the chocolate and mix it gently into the mascarpone. Place the mix in the fridge to firm up until needed.

And finally...

Cut the tart into six equal pieces and place them on six large serving plates. Place a spoon of the mascarpone on top of the thick end of the tart. Lay two pieces of the pineapple in front of the mascarpone and a raspberry to the side. Spoon the syrup over the top of the tart and down the sides. Lay a chocolate scroll on top of the mascarpone and finish with a sprig of mint.

CHEESE

As organisers of the world's greatest dog show, we want to ensure our visitors and dog exhibitors are well looked after. This is the 18th year we've held Crufts at The NEC and the catering team there continues to be innovative with its offering each year – from champagne bars and our exclusive Patron's Club restaurant, to the choice of great fresh food available in their own catering outlets within the halls we utilise.

Catherine Choules
Event Manager, The Kennel Club

Oxford Blue with Port Wine Pears, Port Sorbet and Redcurrant Jam

An interesting and delicious variation on the classic Port and blue cheese marriage…

Port Sorbet

1 cinnamon stick

200ml water

175g caster sugar

200ml Port wine

Port Sorbet

Place the cinnamon stick, water, sugar and port in a small saucepan and heat until the sugar dissolves. Remove from the heat and allow to cool before placing in a clean bowl. Once it's cool, put it in the fridge to chill further. Put the sorbet mixture in an ice cream machine. Churn the mixture until it is almost firm, then transfer to a suitable container and place in the freezer until needed. You can make this well in advance if you want to.

Port Wine Pears

150ml Port wine

150g sugar

1 cinnamon stick

1 orange, halved

1 lemon, halved

3 conference pears, sliced in half
 lengthways

Port Wine Pears

Put all the ingredients in a medium saucepan and bring to the boil, before simmering for 5 minutes. Allow the pears to cool down in the liquor so they take on more of the port flavour. When they're cool, remove from the pan. Cut a thin slice off the bottom of each of the pears so they can lie flat when you put them on a plate.

Redcurrant Jam

200g redcurrant jelly

40ml red wine

2 tbsp honey

Redcurrant Jam

Combine all the ingredients in a saucepan and heat until they are blended. Remove from the pan, allow to cool and place into a squeezy bottle until needed.

Sun-dried Tomato Croute

1 small sun-dried tomato foccacia loaf
1 tbsp extra-virgin olive oil
1 tbsp dried mixed herbs
Sea salt
Cracked black pepper

And finally…

500g Oxford Blue cheese

Sun-dried Tomato Croute

Pre-heat the oven to 160°C. Slice the tomato foccacia into six thin slices and lay them on a piece of greaseproof paper. Drizzle with olive oil, sprinkle with the mixed herbs, sea salt and cracked black pepper. Bake in the oven for 12 minutes until they're golden brown. Remove from the oven and allow to cool.

And finally…

Take the pear halves, remove the inner core and seeds with a teaspoon, and lay them on six medium serving plates with the exposed core facing you.

Cut the Oxford Blue into six equal pieces and place one on top of each pear. Remove the sorbet from the freezer and, using an ice cream scoop, place six scoops of sorbet into small shot glasses or directly on to the plate next to the pear.

Pour the redcurrant jam around the edge of half the plate and lay the croute up the side of the cheese.

Roquefort and William Pear Salad with Caramelised Walnuts and Honey Dressing

A classic combination that looks and tastes fabulous…

Pear Salad

300g lamb's lettuce
1 curly endive
150g red chard
3 William pears
Juice of ½ a lemon
250g Roquefort cheese

Honey Dressing

1 tbsp Dijon mustard
250ml sunflower oil
60ml natural honey

Pear Salad

Tear and wash the salad leaves. Drain them thoroughly and set on some kitchen roll to remove any excess water. Cut each pear in half lengthways, then cut each half into six slices, removing any inner core and seeds. Place in a bowl with lemon juice and a little water to stop them discolouring.

Roughly break the Roquefort into 1cm pieces and set them aside until they're needed.

Honey Dressing

Place the mustard in a large mixing bowl and slowly whisk in the sunflower oil a little at a time. If you add the oil too quickly the dressing will split. When you have reached the desired thickness – that of a classic vinaigrette – whisk in the honey and leave to one side until needed.

Caramelised Walnuts

160g walnuts, peeled
150g caster sugar

And finally…

6 small pieces of chervil

Caramelised Walnuts

Break the walnuts in half. Put the caster sugar and 1 tbsp of water in a non-stick pan and heat until the sugar starts to go light brown. Add the walnut pieces and cook for 1 minute, mixing to ensure they're completely coated. Remove the pan from the heat and carefully remove the walnuts with a fork. Lay them on to a piece of greaseproof paper until they're cool.

And finally…

Divide the salad leaves between six small serving bowls or plates. Drain the pears well, then arrange six per plate around the outside, so they stick up a little. Place the cheese and caramelised walnuts over the lettuce. Drizzle the dressing over the top and finish with a piece of chervil.

Ragstone Goat's Cheese Soufflé with Red Pepper Relish and Red Onion Chutney Spring Rolls

This rather special chutney and soufflé make a perfect creative cheese course…

Red Pepper Relish

2 large red onions, finely chopped
400g red pepper, de-seeded and
  chopped small
200ml malt vinegar
100g granulated sugar

Red Pepper Relish

Put the onions, pepper and vinegar in a large non-stick pot and slowly bring to the boil. Turn down the heat and simmer for 15 minutes or until the peppers are tender.

Add the sugar and bring it back to the boil, stirring to dissolve the sugar. Simmer for 5 minutes until the relish is thick. Remove from the heat, allow to cool and then refrigerate until it's needed.

Red Onion Chutney Spring Rolls

1 red onion, chopped
200ml malt vinegar
1 tsp dried chillies
250g plum tomatoes, skinned
  and chopped
125g cooking apples, peeled, cored
  and chopped small
100g Demerara sugar
50g sultanas
6 large sheets of spring roll pastry
2 egg yolks, beaten

Red Onion Chutney Spring Rolls

Place the onions, vinegar, chillies, tomatoes and apples in a pot. Bring to the boil and simmer for 20 minutes.

Add the sugar and sultanas and stir until the sugar has dissolved. Gently simmer the chutney for 30 minutes, mixing it every now and again to prevent it sticking. The chutney should be thick with no water residue on top. Remove from the pot and place in a clean container and refrigerate until needed.

Pre-heat a deep-fat fryer to 180°C. Take a piece of spring roll pastry and trim the edges until roughly 15cm square. Place 2 tbsp of the chutney mix at one end of the pastry, leaving 1.5cm of pastry at either side. Brush all the sides with egg wash and roll the pastry halfway up.

Fold over the sides, brush the folded sides and the top of the pastry with more egg wash, then continue rolling so the ends become sealed and it becomes a long, thin spring roll. Repeat the process until you have six spring rolls. Place the spring rolls in the fryer and cook for 3 minutes or until golden brown. Remove from the fryer and keep them warm.

Béchamel Sauce

1 litre milk, full fat
100g butter
100g plain flour
1 onion, studded with a clove

Ragstone Goat's Cheese Soufflé

100ml béchamel sauce
2 egg yolks
60g Ragstone goat's cheese, softened
25g melted butter
50g white breadcrumbs
6 egg whites
60g Ragstone goat's cheese, diced
Salt & pepper

Béchamel Sauce

Melt the butter in a thick-bottomed pan. Add the flour and mix it in. Cook for a few minutes over a gentle heat without colouring. Gradually add the warmed milk and stir until smooth. Add the onion and allow to simmer for 30 minutes. Remove the onion, then pass the sauce through a fine strainer.

Ragstone Goat's Cheese Soufflé

Pre-heat the oven to 170°C. Remove the béchamel sauce from the heat, leave for 3 minutes then mix in the egg yolks and goat's cheese. Take six 5cm metal rings and brush the inside with melted butter. Coat the inside of the ring generously with the breadcrumbs. Line a baking tray with parchment paper and lay the six metal rings on top.

In a large mixing bowl, whisk the egg whites until they form stiff peaks. Add a pinch of salt and mix 2 tablespoons of the whisked egg whites into the béchamel mix to loosen it up. Fold the remaining egg whites gently into the béchamel mix.

Half fill the metal rings with the béchamel mix. Divide the diced goat's cheese equally between the metal rings and then pour the rest of the béchamel mix into the top of the rings. Place them on a baking tray and bake in the oven for 10 minutes. Let them stand for 15 minutes and remove the metal rings. Place them back in the oven and cook for a further 5 minutes. Remove from the oven and keep them warm.

And finally…

Place the goat's cheese soufflés to one edge of six medium serving plates. Place a metal ring on the opposite side of the plate and half fill it with the red pepper relish. Remove the ring, then lay the spring roll up the side of the soufflé.

Ashed Chevreaux with Piccallili, Foccacia Croute and Red Beet Vinaigrette

Vibrant colours and a mix of strong flavours make this cheese course so appealing...

Focaccia Croute

1 medium focaccia loaf
1 tbsp extra-virgin olive oil
1 tbsp dried mixed herbs
Salt & pepper

Focaccia Croute

Pre-heat the oven to 160°C. Cut the focaccia into six thin slices and lay them on greaseproof paper on a baking sheet. Drizzle with olive oil and sprinkle with the mixed herbs and salt & pepper. Bake in the oven for 12 minutes until golden brown. Allow to cool.

Piccallili

200g cauliflower, diced
2 carrots, peeled and diced
2 white onions
1 tsp salt
½ cucumber, de-seeded
1 courgette
100g caster sugar
2 tsp ground turmeric
1 tbsp cornflour
1 tsp mustard powder
200ml white wine vinegar
100ml malt vinegar

Piccallili

Cut the cauliflower and carrots into small pieces. Peel and cut the onions into 1cm pieces. Place in a bowl, spinkle with salt and leave to stand for 2-3 hours.

Afterwards, rinse in cold water and dry. Peel and de-seed the cucumber and courgette and cut into 1cm pieces. Dry and add to the cauliflower mix.

Put the sugar, turmeric, cornflour and mustard powder in a small bowl and mix together with a little of the vinegar to form a paste. Bring the vinegars to the boil in a small pan, add the paste and cook for 1 minute. Pour the mix over the vegetables. Place in a bowl and refrigerate until needed.

Red Beet Vinaigrette

250g beetroot
1 sprig thyme
2 cloves of garlic, crushed
100ml red wine
50g granulated sugar
50ml balsamic vinegar

Red Beet Vinaigrette

Put the beetroot, thyme and garlic into a medium saucepan, cover with water and bring to the boil. Simmer for 30 minutes and remove from the heat. Using a hand blender, blitz the mix until it's smooth and pass it through a fine strainer into a bowl.

Place the red wine, sugar and balsamic vinegar in a separate saucepan and bring to the boil. Reduce the mixture by half; this should take around 10 minutes. Add it to the beetroot mix. If the vinaigrette is too thin, place it back on the stove and reduce further until you have the desired thickness.

Refrigerate and transfer to a squeezy bottle until needed.

And finally…

6 x 120g Ashed Chevreaux
  goat's cheese
120g curly endive, torn

And finally…

Place a 5cm metal ring on six medium serving plates. Fill the rings a quarter of the way up with piccallili mix and then remove the rings. Lay the goat's cheese on top of the piccallili and set some of the curly endive on top. Place a foccacia croute on top of the lettuce and dot the red beet vinaigrette around the plate.

STOCKS & SAUCES

To make six portions of any stock or sauce is very difficult. That's why all our recipes are based on at least 800ml-1.5 litres, which allows the cooking process to capture the correct flavour. Whatever you don't use should be left to cool down, then placed in the fridge – it can be used within two to three days. Alternatively, you can freeze them into smaller quantities (using an ice cube tray is a great idea) and they can be kept up to three months.

Vegetable Stock

(Makes approx 1.5 litres)

3 tbsp extra-virgin olive oil

4 white onions, peeled and roughly chopped

2 celery sticks, trimmed and chopped

1 large leek, cleaned and roughly chopped

Half a head of garlic, split

½ tsp black peppercorns

1 bay leaf

2 litres water

1 sprig fresh tarragon

1 tbsp fresh parsley

1 sprig thyme

1 sprig basil

½ tsp white peppercorns

240ml dry white wine

Seasoning

Vegetable Stock

Heat the olive oil in a large saucepan. Add all the vegetables, garlic and peppercorns and cook until soft. Add the water and the bay leaf, then bring to the boil and simmer for 25 minutes and reduce by a quarter until you have approximately 1.75 litres of stock. Remove the pan from the heat and then add all the herbs, white wine and a little seasoning. Give the stock a good stir, so all the herbs are infused, and leave for 20 minutes. Strain through a fine sieve and allow to cool rapidly.

Chicken Stock

(Makes approx 1.5 litres)

2 tbsp olive oil

2 large carrots, roughly chopped

2 onions, peeled and chopped

1 celery stick

1 leek, cleaned and chopped

4 cloves of garlic, peeled

2 bay leaves

1 sprig thyme

2 tbsp tomato purée

2 tbsp plain flour

1.5kg chicken bones

2.5 litres water

Salt & pepper

Chicken Stock

Heat the olive oil in a large saucepan. Add the vegetables, garlic, bay leaves and thyme and cook over a medium heat, ensuring the vegetables are cooked without any colour. Stir in the tomato purée and flour and cook for another minute.

Add the chicken bones and cover with the water, then lightly season. Bring to the boil and skim off any froth that rises to the top. Lower the heat to a simmer and leave to cook gently for an hour. Remove from the heat.

Let the stock cool down for 30 minutes before passing it through a fine strainer or sieve.

Brown Chicken Stock

(Makes approx 1.5 litres)

2 tbsp olive oil

2 large carrots, roughly chopped

2 onions, peeled and chopped

1 celery stick, trimmed and chopped

1 large leek, cleaned and chopped

4 cloves of garlic, peeled

2 bay leaves

1 sprig thyme

2 tbsp tomato purée

2 tbsp plain flour

1.5kg chicken bones

3 litres water

Salt & pepper

Brown Chicken Stock

Pre-heat the oven to 170°C. Place the chicken bones in a large roasting tin, and roast in the oven until golden brown. Heat the olive oil in a large saucepan, then add the vegetables, garlic, bay leaves and thyme and cook over a medium heat, ensuring the vegetables are cooked to a dark caramel colour. Stir in the tomato purée and flour and cook for another minute. Add the roasted chicken bones and cover with the water, then lightly season. Bring to the boil and skim off any froth that rises to the top. Lower the heat to a simmer and leave to cook gently for an hour. Remove from the heat. Let the stock cool down for 30 minutes before passing it through a fine strainer or sieve.

Fish Stock

(Makes approx 1.5 litres)

1.5kg fish bones (halibut or sole)

1 tbsp extra-virgin olive oil

1 large leek, cleaned and chopped

1 celery stalk, chopped

1 large onion, peeled

4 cloves of garlic

1 small fennel bulb, peeled and chopped

150ml white wine

2 sprigs parsley

1.5 litres water

Salt & pepper

Fish Stock

Wash the fish bones and break the larger ones in half. Roughly chop the vegetables. Heat the olive oil in a large saucepan and add the chopped vegetables. Slowly cook them with the garlic, without browning. Continually stir for about 5 minutes.

Add the fish bones, white wine and parsley and bring to the boil and reduce the wine by half, before pouring in the cold water and bringing it to the boil. Skim off the froth, lower the heat and simmer for 20 minutes. Remove the pan from the heat and allow the stock to settle for 20 minutes, then pass through a fine sieve and season to taste.

Fish Velouté

(Makes approx 1 litre)

80g salted butter

80g flour

1 litre fish stock, hot

Juice of 1 lemon

Salt & pepper

200ml double cream

Fish Velouté

Heat the butter in a medium saucepan until it's melted. Add the flour and mix together to create a roux. Gradually add the warm fish stock to the roux, stirring continuously with a wooden spoon to prevent it from catching on the bottom or becoming lumpy. Cook gently, stirring continuously, over a low heat for 20 minutes. Remove from the heat and pass through a fine strainer, then add the lemon juice and season to taste. When you need to use the sauce, finish with a little cream to give the sauce a more creamy consistency.

Red Wine Sauce

(Makes approx 800ml)

2 tbsp olive oil

40g shallots, peeled and finely chopped

40g carrots, finely chopped

40g celery, finely chopped

½ tsp black peppercorns

1 clove of garlic, crushed

500ml red wine

1 litre brown chicken stock

1 sprig thyme

1 bay leaf

1 tsp red wine vinegar

25g unsalted butter

Salt & pepper

Red Wine Sauce

Heat the olive oil in a large saucepan. Add the shallots and all the chopped vegetables and garlic and cook over a medium heat until they're lightly browned. Add the peppercorns, thyme, bay leaf and vinegar. Pour in the red wine, bring it to the boil and boil the liquor rapidly until it's reduced by half and takes on a rich syrupy consistency.

Add the brown chicken stock, boil until the sauce has reduced by half again, then remove from the heat, add the butter, a little at a time, and strain through a fine sieve. Season to taste.

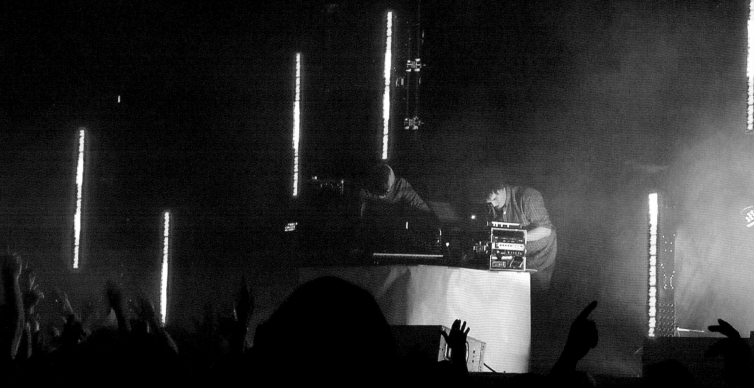

FROM MEAT LOAF TO A BANQUET FOR 2,000

The talented chefs at The NEC Group create delicious meals for more than four million visitors a year, with many well-known celebrities among them. Rod Stewart, Tom Jones, Meat Loaf, Bryan Adams and Diana Ross have all dined at its venues, alongside cabinet ministers, heads of state, diplomats and members of the Royal Family...

For music fans attending concerts, fashion enthusiasts visiting the Clothes Show Live, or for business conference delegates or international traders, the dedicated team of chefs working across The NEC Group's venues ensures every menu is tailor-made.

While every show has its own combination of dishes, The NEC Group's core catering ethos is based on a blend of simplicity, experience and innovation, with fresh ingredients, inspired flavours and mouth-watering presentation coming together to create appealing dishes.

With 30 years' experience of setting the stage for some of the UK's best-loved shows, some of the world's most important business events and the very best in live music, it's no surprise that The NEC Group's chefs have collected more than 300 catering awards.

The NEC Group has 63 kitchens spread across its four world-class venues – The NEC (National Exhibition Centre), LG Arena, The NIA (National Indoor Arena) and The ICC (International Convention Centre) – as well as The REP Conference & Banqueting Centre in Birmingham city centre.

The NEC

With 200,000 square metres of covered exhibition space through 21 interconnected halls – unparalleled in the UK – The NEC is the UK's largest exhibition venue and the busiest in Europe. Often described as an exhibition 'village', The NEC site is set in 650 acres of parkland just eight miles from Birmingham city centre, and has its own network of roads, four on-site hotels, a lake, 21,000 car parking spaces, plus security, traffic and fire-fighting teams. The adjacent Birmingham International rail station and airport, along with the M42 and M6 motorways, provide visitors with quick and convenient access to The NEC, from across the country and internationally.

Alongside the three million human visitors that pass through the doors each year, The NEC welcomes 250,000 dogs to Crufts, the world's largest dog show, and a staggering 1,600 horses to the prestigious *Horse of the Year Show*. With such a busy calendar of show activity, The NEC's 70 catering outlets alone serve 1,500,000 cups of tea, 2,500,000 cups of coffee, 2,800 bottles of champagne and 75,000 bottles of beer and lager every year!

To meet the ever-increasing demand from visitors, exhibitors and organisers, catering at The NEC has become a more important part of the visitor experience. Over the last three years, catering has seen a £10 million investment, which has included refurbishment of 12 in-hall catering outlets, with six more planned for 2008/2009.

Launched under the banner 'NEC food', the team is serving even more enticing menus in stylish surroundings. The restaurants have been completely refurbished, providing visitors with relaxing, comfortable, contemporary environments. From a full three-course meal to soup or a sandwich on the move, The NEC dining experience offers a variety of restaurant styles to suit every visitor, providing choice depending on what their taste buds are telling them.

The team also takes its corporate responsibilities seriously and has introduced a series of initiatives, including the introduction of fully bio-degradable packaging across its range of take-away sandwiches.

LG Arena and The NIA

LG Arena and The NIA are two of Europe's busiest arenas, offering an unrivalled range of concerts, entertainment and sporting events, from Take That to Disney on Ice and Crufts to the World Indoor Athletics Championships.

LG Arena located on The NEC site is perhaps best known for regularly hosting spectacular sell-out concerts to suit all musical tastes, from Rod Stewart and Kylie Minogue to Foo Fighters and Muse. The venue is also home to the Horse of the Year Show and several international trade fairs and conferences.

The NIA, located in Birmingham city centre, has established itself as the UK's home of indoor sport, providing a stage for the world's élite competitors and a platform for rising stars at events such as Davis Cup tennis, European Indoor Athletics Championships and World Badminton Championships. It also provides the perfect showcase for world-class entertainment such as Little Britain, Cirque du Soleil, Lee Evans and Bill Bailey.

Visitors to both arenas can enjoy a pre-event dining experience at the group's members-only hospitality club – getting a fantastic night out off to a great start.

The ICC

The ICC is one of Europe's leading conference venues, offering an extensive range of first-class facilities. With 11 halls, 10 executive meeting rooms and a team of experienced professionals, The ICC hosts more than 500 events a year.

Since opening in 1991, The ICC has been recognised with a broad range of high-profile industry awards, including Best Conference and Banqueting Staff and the title Best UK Conference Venue, an accolade it has won consistently over many years.

Together, The ICC and its in-house catering team offer the flexibility and resources to welcome several thousand delegates to everything from AGMs and international conferences to high-profile banquets and executive meetings. No matter what the event, the team is able to rise to almost any request, and with the introduction of a restaurant-style definitive choice menu, guests can even now select their meals at the table.

Our mission

Over the last three years, The NEC Group has been on a journey to transform catering at our venues for everyone: visitors, exhibitors and organisers alike, by developing every aspect of service, presentation and performance. The new catering concepts give visitors the opportunity to taste the wide selection of great food on offer, and enjoy a choice of dining options to suit their individual tastes.

Ultimately, The NEC Group catering team aims to set the benchmark for catering excellence across the live events and exhibition industry by putting food first. Across the venues, the team of gifted chefs and their combination of innovation and passion continues to provide a recipe for success, taking food at The Group's venues from good to great and on to world-class.

It also operates one of the UK's premium outdoor and fixed site event caterers, Amadeus (www.amadeusfood.co.uk), which provides a range of fine dining and public catering for some of the UK's most prestigious events. These include the Barclays Scottish Open Golf tournament, the Embassy World Snooker Championships and the Cirque du Soleil Saltimbanco.

THE NEC GROUP TEAM

The team at The NEC Group is made up of some very talented individuals, whose expertise delivers over 900 exhibitions, conferences, concerts, entertainment, sporting events and stand-alone banquets every year. Each and every event requires input from all of our teams. From sales specialists, stewards and event planners to box office experts, rigging technicians and catering staff, we recognise that teamwork is key to delivering a successful event.

While this book is in celebration and recognition of the skill of so many of our talented and dedicated chefs, who – during spring 2008 alone – won more than 30 awards at a number of prestigious national and international competitions, it is also a chance for us to acknowledge the commitment, ability and professionalism that each of our NEC Group employees demonstrates, each and every day.

The accolades collected by our Group chefs included seven gold medals, three silver, 12 bronze and six certificates of merit at four prestigious competitions: Le Salon Culinaire International de Londres, incorporating the British Open Cookery Championships; the Wessex Salon Culinaire; the MARCHE awards; and the Food & Drinks Expo 2008.

At Le Salon Culinaire International de Londres, The NEC Group also won the illustrious Rational Master Chefs Grand Prix at silver standard, beating teams from Claridge's London and the Compass Culinary Team.

Ultimately, we aim to set the benchmark for catering excellence across the live events and exhibition industry by putting our food first and developing every aspect of what we do from good to great and on to world class. Collecting awards is just one way of demonstrating that we are leading the way.

BIOGRAPHIES

Along with continual support and encouragement from Chief Executive Paul Thandi and his Executive Board team, a number of key senior managers within the catering department have made the production of this book possible.

Sally Davis

Managing Director, The NEC Group Catering

As a member of The NEC Group Executive Board, and MD of Group Catering, Sally is responsible for 250 permanent staff, 1,000 casual staff and a turnover of approximately £30million. Her role is to lead a large food and beverage team, including a food factory, high-profile conference and banqueting business, retail catering and Amadeus, the Group's premium outdoor catering division. Sally is a consummate brand champion. A key focus has been to set the departmental strategy and ensure high-level planning enables recognition for her team's ability to take niche, quality products, service and delivery and adapt them for volume catering environments.

Earl Withers

Operations Director, The NEC Group Catering

Earl manages a team of four operational general managers and two support managers across the business and is tasked with ensuring excellent operational standards and maximum financial performance. He is also a vital link between The NEC, The ICC, LG Arena and The NIA management teams; co-ordinating long-term resource and maintenance planning. Earl's passion is for people and ensuring his team has the resource and capability to deliver the UK's best catering at the UK's best venues.

Mary Amos

Purchasing Manager, The NEC Group Catering

Mary is responsible for purchasing, administration and warehousing within catering across the Group and has, in recent years, headed project teams for a number of large-scale ventures, such as the replacement of the till systems and, most recently, replacement of the back office system for managing stock and sales.

Neil Ashton

Deputy Executive Chef, The NEC

Neil's role manages 33 full-time chefs who work across 31 kitchens delivering fine dining, and hospitality and production work. He is also responsible for liaising with the key account management team to write bespoke menus for themed or unusual events.

Simon Beattie

General Manager – Catering, The NEC

Simon is responsible for all catering on The NEC site, incorporating a team of four who deliver catering operations for key accounts, exhibitions and conference and banqueting, as well as liaison between The NEC and its retail service partners.

Allan Boyle

General Manager – Catering, The ICC

Allan leads a diverse team from head chefs to conference and banqueting managers at one of Europe's leading convention centres. He is responsible for ensuring a consistently high standard of conference catering and banqueting delivery and also for the success of the venue's retail outlet, Cafe Vite.

Susan Cardno

Commercial Finance Manager, The NEC Group Catering

Susan leads a team of commercial accountants to provide extensive financial performance information and also acts as a business advisor to help develop the department's strategic direction.

Jayne Devlin

General Manager – Amadeus and The REP Conference and Banqueting Centre

Jayne's role encompasses winning new business, negotiating contracts and developing the reputation of the recently re-launched premium outdoor catering division, Amadeus, as well as leading an operational management team at The REP Centre and at outside events.

Wendy Hallam

Resources and Training Manager, The NEC Group Catering

Wendy has overall responsibility for staffing, recruitment and development within catering across the Group, encompassing The NEC, The ICC, LG Arena, The NIA, Wine REPublic and Amadeus. Her role also includes managing large-scale projects and working closely with operational teams to ensure we secure the right people for the events side of our business.

Mike Jeyes

Executive Head Chef, City Centre venues

Mike heads a group of chefs over the three city centre sites, ensuring consistently high quality of food for a wide audience profile. Mike has developed the banqueting offer over the years from silver to plated service and introduced a groundbreaking concept – a restaurant-style choice of menu to guests at the table for up to 1,000 guests.

Carol Lohoar

Senior Health & Hygiene Manager, The NEC Group Catering

Carol's role extends across all the Group venues. She is charged with maintaining high levels of departmental safety and ensuring synergy across the venues through a food safety management system and review audits. Carol manages three fully qualified food and safety support team members.

Caryn Masters

General Manager – Catering, LG Arena and The NIA

Caryn's role seeks to align the management of the catering operations at both of the arena venues with the Group arena vision. Caryn leads a team of Arena Catering Managers who deliver a range of products – from premium hospitality to public catering units.

Cyril Wilkins

Commissary Manager, The NEC

Cyril is responsible for new product development, as well as ensuring retail units within the exhibition halls and the on-stand catering service have a selection of high quality fresh products and snack items available, as well as providing buffet items to hospitality areas within the Group venues.

Caroline Young

Business Development Manager, The NEC Group Catering

Caroline's role seeks to drive the development of existing business as well as new opportunities across all catering business units through relevant research and analysis. She is also responsible for the coordination of the Group Catering marketing strategy.

Le Salon Culinaire International de Londres, 17-21 February 2008

The renowned Salon Culinaire is the UK's largest internationally respected chefs' competition, which served more than 85 competition classes over five days.

List of medals received NEC Group chefs:

Adrian Ford – Gold, Show Platter of Fish (Best in Class Award)

John Berry – Gold, Miniature Pastillage

Daniel Tennant – Gold, Junior Meat Platter (Best in Class Award and Special Award, Best in Category)

Tony Morrin – Silver, Hotelympia Fish Dish Challenge

John Berry – Silver, Works in Fat

Matthew Burr – Silver, Grand Masterclass (Gastro Pub)

Kevin Megee – Bronze, Show Platter of Meat

Paul Connolly – Bronze, Figgjo Masterclass

Stuart Garbett – Bronze, Figgjo Masterclass

From The ICC, six bronze medals for Parade des chefs:

Mike Jeyes, Simon Hellier, Andy Redmond, Matt Eades, Leon Churchill, Aaron Ward

Donna Nicholson – Merit, The British Pepper & Spice "Millstone" Ethnic Class

Julie Davis – Merit, Pastillage Mask

Wessex Salon Culinaire, 11-12 March 2008

The 2008 Wessex Salon Culinaire is recognised as one of the leading competitions for up-and-coming chefs.

List of medals received by The NEC Group chefs:

Adrian Ford – Gold, Prawn starter

Paul Bertram – Bronze, Avocado starter

Donna Nicholson – Bronze, Fish dish

Carl Thompson – Merit, Hot plated chocolate dessert

Steven Stack – Merit, Lamb dish

MARCHE awards, 16 March 2008

The MARCHE awards – the academy awards of the region's restaurant, catering, hotel and bar trade – were held at The ICC on 16 March.

List of medals received by The NEC Group staff:

Chris le Friec – Fine Dining Assistant of the Year

Wayne Round – Drinks Service Assistant of the Year

Carl Thompson – Chef of the Year – Silver Award

Food & Drinks Expo 2008, 6-9 April 2008

Food & Drink Expo 2008 is the UK's leading food and drink trade show, held at The NEC in Birmingham.

List of medals received by The NEC Group chefs:

Jason Taws – Gold (and best in class), Lamb dish

John O'Reily – Gold, Two-course lunch in bowls

Tony Morrin – Gold, Two-course lunch in bowls

Matthew Burr – Bronze, Gastro Pub

Paul Bertram – Certificate of Merit, Warm salad

Donna Nicholson – Certificate of Merit, British produce

CONVERSION CHART

METRIC WEIGHTS

1 kilogramme	=	2.2046lb	=	2lbs 3¼oz
7 grammes	=	¼oz		
14 grammes	=	½oz		
21 grammes	=	¾oz		
28 grammes	=	1oz		
453½ grammes	=	1lb		

FLUIDS

1 litre	=	35 fluid oz	=	1¾ pints
½ litre	=	17½ fluid oz		
1 litre	=	1000cc (or ml - millilitres)		

ENGLISH MEASURES

1 pint	=	20 fluid oz	=	568cc
1 gill	=	5 fluid oz (¼ pint)	=	142cc
Bottle table wine	=	24 fluid oz	=	680cc
1 pound (lb)	=	16oz		

OVEN TEMPERATURES

	Electric °F	Gas	Centigrade equivalent
Cool oven	225 - 250	0 - ½	7 - 121
Very slow oven	250 - 275	½ - 1	121 - 135
Slow oven	275 - 300	1 - 2	135 - 149
Very moderate oven	300 - 350	2 - 3	149 - 177
Moderate oven	375	4	190
Moderately hot oven	400	5	204
Hot oven	425 - 450	6 - 7	218 - 233
Very hot oven	475 - 500	8 - 9	246 - 260

OTHER MEASUREMENTS

2 teaspoons	=	1 dessertspoon
2 dessertspoons	=	1 tablespoon
6 tablespoons	=	1 teacup
2 tablespoons water	=	½ gill
1 teacup	=	1 gill (or 5 fl oz)
1 breakfast cup	=	½ pint
1 tablespoon dry substance	=	1 ounce
1 dessertspoon butter	=	1 ounce
1 breakfast cup flour	=	½ pound
1 pint flour	=	1 pound

INDEX

MY THANKS TO…

Sally Davis, Managing Director, Group Catering, for having the unshakable belief and vision that her team of chefs could produce a book that captures our customers' imaginations and the spirit of what our department is all about.

James Brown, Head of Marketing, and his team for their advice, guidance and hours of commitment to perfection.

Anthony Barlow, who laboriously typed most of the manuscript with a smile on his face and never failed to bring humour to this challenge.

Paul Connolly, who prepared each of the dishes used in the photoshoot, capturing the essence of this book.

John Berry and Julie Davis – my two pastry chefs – who took recipes normally used for hundreds and converted them into dinner party-friendly recipes for six.

Michelle Agnew, my secretary, who – with the patience of a saint and on top of her normal workload – had the thankless task of ensuring every member of the book team delivered to deadline.

Huge thanks go to Tina Boughey, for styling the food so beautifully and to Andy Davis for capturing it all so perfectly on camera. I'd also like to thank our publisher, Modus Creative, for their stylish design and editing of this book.

Neil Ashton, Kevin Megee, Mike Jeyes, Simon Hellier, Steve McCarthy, Tony Morrin and all the chefs who work across The NEC Group for their support, ideas, vision and dedication in bringing this book to life.

The many talented and inspirational chefs with whom I have worked with over the years and have formed my brigade at The NEC Group.

You are only as good as the team allows you to be…